DAILY GOSPEL

By the same author

AFTER MIDNIGHT

CHURCH AFLAME

HEADLINE PULPIT

NAKED TRUTH

WORLD CONQUEST

PERILOUS TIMES

OTHER GOSPELS

EASTWARD TO MOSCOW

THE QUESTION OF SOUTH AFRICA

THE CHURCH ON THE BRINK

THE SENDERS

JESUS, BY JOHN

DAILY GOSPEL

EVANGELISTIC MEDITATIONS FOR EVERY DAY
OF THE YEAR

by

PAUL B. SMITH, B.A., D.D.

WELCH PUBLISHING COMPANY INC.
Burlington, Ontario, Canada

Formerly published (1963) by Zondervan Publishing House,
Grand Rapids, Michigan, and (1965) by Marshall, Morgan and Scott, Ltd.,
London, England.

ISBN: 0-919532-60-8

G.R. Welch Company, Limited
960 Gateway
Burlington, Ontario
L7L 5K7 Canada

© 1980 G.R. Welch Company, Limited

Printed in Canada

PREFACE

The most difficult people to reach with the Gospel are our own children and our close friends.

There is something about an intimate relationship that makes it hard to talk about spiritual matters. Perhaps it is because we tend to take spiritual matters for granted in those who are near and dear to us. I have met many fathers who are fervent witnesses to the world but have never felt free to explain the way of salvation to their children. This is true of some of the most spiritual people I know.

Daily Gospel is written in an attempt to fill this gap. It gives us a short reading for every day of the year. It is not merely devotional but rather it is evangelistic. It is designed to become a part of our family worship. Read whatever we would normally use for this important part of the family life of all Christian homes, and then in one minute add to it the *Daily Gospel* reading for the day. In this way, without preaching at our families or our friends, we have automatically included in our Family Worship a direct evangelistic message.

This is for Christian families where so often there are loved ones and friends sitting with us at the table who have been in an orthodox atmosphere all their lives but have never made their own decisions for Christ.

In these messages I have approached the gospel message from almost every conceivable standpoint. Logic, love, judgment, heaven, hell, challenge, transformation, and scores of other elements of the Good News are stressed. In some cases I have dwelt upon the qualities of a real Christian or his obligations and responsibilities, as a means of establishing a contrast between the saved and the unsaved in the minds of the readers.

For the sake of the meticulous Bible student I should explain that occasionally I have used "proof texts" and deliberately taken them out of their immediate contexts. However, in the few instances where this occurs I have been careful not to use any passage or verse out of context with the teaching of the whole Bible on that particular subject. References appear with the quotations and may be read aloud — or not — as the devotional leader chooses.

These small sermons include more than 545 different verses of Scripture taken from fifty-one books of the Bible. There is little repetition apart from the actual explanations of the way of salvation. There is only one way of salvation and a limited number of different ways that it may be worded.

It is my hope that *Daily Gospel* will eventually find its way into the Family Worship of the Christians of the world and result in the evangelization of the people who are so hard to reach — our immediate families and our close friends.

Toronto, Canada — PAUL B. SMITH

JAN. 1

This is the day that a man usually chooses to turn over a new leaf and start living a better life. This is good, but this is not Christianity. When a man trusts Jesus Christ as his Saviour, not only is the future assured, but the sins of the past are taken care of as well. Christianity does not involve the turning over of a new leaf, but the birth of a new life.

The Bible says, "Therefore, if any man be in Christ, he is a new creature: old things are passed away; behold, all things are become new" (II Corinthians 5:17).

Most of us have tried the new leaf, and it has failed. What we need is a new life.

JAN. 2

Down through human history there have been many great leaders who have moved men in the right direction. There have been some outstanding examples that have inspired others in their achievements. There have been scientists who have delved into the secrets of nature and learned facts that have made life easier. Occasionally a dedicated physician has been able to uncover truths that have improved the entire world's physical condition.

To all of these pioneers and prophets we owe a debt of gratitude, but none of them has been able to meet our greatest need — a Saviour. A Saviour who can break the bonds of sin, remove the stains of wickedness, fill the void of godlessness, and regenerate our dead spiritual beings.

The work of Jesus Christ begins where the best efforts of the great must disappear into the darkness of the unknown and the impossible. The Bible says: "Thou shalt call his name Jesus: for He shall save his people from their sins" (Matthew 1:21).

JAN.
3
It is more difficult to please man than God. When the real test comes man is short of patience and grace and forgiveness. He has a tendency to be lenient to a point and then vindictive. He allows for a certain amount of sin but there are areas of unrighteousness that man never forgives. He can reach only so far toward the degenerate but there is a level of degeneracy that man considers beyond the reach of any helping hand.

The Bible states that as far as God is concerned there will be an end of the day of grace and the beginning of the day of judgment, but meanwhile no one is too bad, too deep, too dirty, too drunk, too immoral, or too corrupt to save. The Bible says: "Though your sins be as scarlet, they shall be as white as snow; though they be red like crimson, they shall be as wool" (Isaiah 1:18).

JAN.
4
Jesus said, "Sell whatsoever thou hast and give to the poor" (Mark 10:21). Communism says, "Sell whatsoever the rich man has, and distribute it among yourselves."

Some people think that Christianity involves a sort of communistic approach to life. If a man sells out and helps the poor, he is a Christian. Of course, everyone knows that Jesus said this to one particular man who had obviously made an idol of his wealth.

However, even to this rich man whose possessions were preventing him from reaching God, Jesus did not stop at this point. He added in the same sentence: "and come, take up the cross, and follow me."

There is no Christian experience that does not start at the foot of the cross and in personal contact with the risen Lord. It is good to distribute to the poor, but what a tragedy to mistake this partial step for the complete step of faith in the Son of God.

JAN. 5

The Gospel makes no distinctions of color or race or cast. It addresses its appeal to the outcast of society who has committed all the crimes in the book. Its door is open to the man whose moral integrity is unimpeachable and whose outward propriety is scrupulous.

During His ministry Jesus met with all classes of people and was able to satisfy their needs. In the Philippian jailer, the lepers, the thief on the cross, and the Gadarean demoniac He dealt with and delivered representatives of the lower strata of society. His contacts with Nicodemus and the rich young ruler demonstrated His power to diagnose the problems of the upper elements of humanity.

The Bible says: "Wherefore he is able also to save them to the uttermost that come unto God by him, seeing he ever liveth to make intercession for them" (Hebrews 7:25).

His power is universal in its scope. The condition upon which it works is also universal. Man must come. Then Christ will save.

JAN. 6

There are three tenses to salvation — past, present, and future.

When a man trusts Christ as his Saviour, he is justified. He is reconciled to God and the sin of the *past* is forgiven and cleansed. As he continues in his Christian life, he is sanctified, or kept by the power of God in the *present*. He looks *forward* to the day when he will be glorified — taken into the personal presence of Christ for eternity.

The Bible says: "It is of the Lord's mercies that we are not consumed, because his compassions fail not" (Lamentations 3:22).

If God had mercy on us while we were sinners, how much more we can depend upon God to finish the work of redemption by keeping us now and forever.

JAN.
7

If I could publish my own Bible, there are many things in this world that I would write out of existence. I would commence with sin and end with death and in between I would also remove the burdens of disease and crime and poverty and war. Perhaps it would be easier on the conscience of us all if in my deified position I could also eradicate the possibility of punishment after death.

However, fortunately I am not God and no other man is God. If we were, in our childish desire to avoid the things we did not like we would make a terrible botch of the whole business. As a Christian, the only authoritative answer I can get to the things I do not understand and cannot control is in the Christian's textbook, the Bible.

The Bible says, "But the fearful, and unbelieving, and the abominable, and murderers, and whoremongers, and sorcerers, and idolaters, and all liars, shall have their part in the lake which burneth with fire and brimstone; which is the second death" (Revelation 21:8).

JAN.
8

There are many names used in the Bible to describe God and each one points up some particular attribute. In the Old Testament He is called a Shepherd and the New Testament carries this name over and applies it directly to Jesus Christ.

With a complete understanding of the Divine significance of the title "Shepherd" Jesus said: "I am the good shepherd: the good shepherd giveth his life for the sheep" (John 10:11).

The most important aspect of God as Shepherd is His voluntary sacrifice for the sins of mankind through the death of Jesus Christ on the cross. There is abundant blessing in the providing and keeping power of God, but the man who has not met the Good Shepherd in His atoning work on Calvary must be forever a stranger to these temporal blessings.

JAN. 9 The Psalmist compares the stability of a righteous man to a tree that has been firmly planted. "He shall be like a tree planted by the rivers of water" (Psalm 1:3).

The Christian is planted as far as his purpose in life is concerned. He has a reason for being alive. He is planted as far as his morality is concerned. His morals do not change with the fashion of the times but are fixed permanently by the Word of God. He is planted as far as his hope for the future is concerned. He knows where he is going and regardless of the immediate obstacles in the course he has his eye set upon the finish mark and knows he will reach it.

In the same Psalm the shiftless nature of the unrighteous man is likened to "the chaff which the wind driveth away" (Psalm 1:4).

He has no reason for existing, he has a sliding scale of morality that moves with the times, and his future is measured only in terms of years with no guarantee even of these.

Our affiliation with Jesus Christ determines whether we are trees planted or chaff blown.

JAN. 10 The gospel of John tells the story of a woman, caught in the act of adultery, who was brought to Jesus by a group of religious men.

She was a sinner. The men knew it, she knew it, and Jesus knew it; but Jesus made it quite clear that the people who brought her were also sinners. She was guilty of adultery. They were guilty of jealousy, hatred, pride, envy. All were sinners in the eyes of God.

The Bible says, "But he that doeth wrong shall receive for the wrong which he hath done: and there is no respect of persons" (Colossians 3:25).

One sinner is not better than another in the eyes of God. All have sinned and all must have a Saviour.

JAN. 11 To become a Christian you believe facts and accept a Person. The Bible says: "He that heareth my word, and believeth on him that sent me, hath everlasting life, and shall not come into condemnation, but is passed from death unto life" (John 5:24).

There are those who know all the facts about Christ. They have heard the Word of God and the way of salvation, but they are not Christians because they have never invited Jesus Christ to come into their lives.

They know the words but not the One who spoke them. They know the way but not the One who showed it. They know the Atonement but not the Person who made it.

Christianity is not a creed, a code, or even a cross. It is a personal relationship with God through faith in the living Lord.

JAN. 12 Everyone must go through a certain amount of trial and tribulation. The Christian life does not keep a man out of trouble, but it does give him the power to go through it and come out on the other side a better man.

Tribulation over a long period of time produces a patience that the average man does not have and a depth of experience which gives the Christian more confidence than he has ever had before.

In tribulation a man has an unparalleled opportunity of proving the sustaining power of his relationship with the Lord.

The Apostle Paul says, "And not only so, but we glory in tribulations also: knowing that tribulation worketh patience; and patience, experience; and experience hope: And hope maketh not ashamed" (Romans 5:3-5).

After a period of trial, the man who knows God can say with confidence, "If God can keep me through this, he can keep me through anything." Tribulation produces hope.

JAN. 13　The woman at the well was physically thirsty but she had no real concept of the parched condition of her spiritual life. She was living in deep sin and the thirst of her soul had been ignored in her quest for physical happiness.

When she met the Master she had an emptiness and dryness on the inside that she had never stopped to question and that she had never understood. Whenever the emptiness became too great to endure she attempted to drown it in her own variety of physical debauchery.

Jesus reminded her of her spiritual need and urged her to drink by faith of the water that would quench her thirst. "But whosoever drinketh of the water that I shall give him shall never thirst; but the water that I shall give him shall be in him a well of water springing up into everlasting life" (John 4:14).

JAN. 14　Sin does not start on a grand scale. It usually commences with an incident that is apparently harmless but inevitably terminates with consequences that are appallingly destructive.

Few people plunge into vile sin all at one time on the impulse of a moment. Great sin is usually the culmination of a series of lesser sins. Gross immorality starts from an impure thought. The bank robber may have his roots in a boy who steals pennies from milk boxes. Embezzlement of the national treasury could originate in a teenager who cheats on his examinations.

The Bible says, "Behold, also the ships, which though they be so great, and are driven of fierce winds, yet are they turned about with a very small helm . . . Even so the tongue is a little member, and boasteth great things. Behold, how great a matter a little fire kindleth!" (James 3:4-5).

JAN. 15 If a stone is thrown into a pool, there is a splash, a ripple, and then nothing.

You and I may make a big splash or a tiny ripple on the sea of this material world, but someday death will fill in the small hole we have made and time will erase the ripples we have left. What will matter then will be where we go after the splash of physical life is over.

The Bible says, "For God so loved the world, that he gave his only begotten Son, that whosoever believeth in him should not perish, but have everlasting life" (John 3:16). Through faith in Christ, God gives us something more to look forward to than the splash of physical life.

JAN. 16 The language of the Bible is the language of everyday life — love, learning, family, food. Each of these in its own way is a sort of human common denominator. Here we all meet despite our superficial differences of race or color or wealth. All of us love someone or something; we learn a great deal in the course of our years; we come from a family and usually produce a family; and everyone must eat.

There are three basic foods mentioned in the Bible — milk, meat, and bread. Each has its spiritual counterpart. Peter told us that milk is the Word of God. Immediately after His talk with the Samaritan woman, Jesus revealed to His disciples that meat is the will of God, and in the same gospel He described Himself as the Bread of Heaven: "I am the living bread which came down from heaven: if any man eat of this bread, he shall live forever" (John 6:51).

The essential thing is not in the fact of knowing about the Bread but in the act of eating it. Eternal life does not come to those who know but to those who eat. This demands more than a mental adjustment. It prescribes an act of faith.

JAN. 17   The rich farmer was an intelligent man. The gospel of Luke says that he used his mental capacities to solve a concrete problem in his life and situation.

Jesus called him a fool, but not because he used his mind. Man is given a certain amount of natural equipment with which to meet the problems of life and there is no promise that God will do for man what He has given him the ability to do for himself. The old adage is good — "The Lord helps those who help themselves."

This man was a fool because he allowed his reasoning powers to take the place of his contact with God. The Bible says, "The fear of the Lord is the beginning of wisdom: and the knowledge of the holy is understanding" (Proverbs 9:10).

JAN. 18   The basic moral laws of God never change. Lying and murder and adultery are just as wrong in the New Testament as in the Old. However, the New Testament recognizes the fact that if man had to depend upon keeping these laws to be saved, it would be impossible. At some point he always breaks down.

Then the New Testament declares the glorious truth that Christ fulfilled the demands of the law when He died on the cross and that man is justified — not because he keeps the law — but through faith in Christ.

The Apostle Paul discusses this whole problem in the third chapter of Romans and finally sums it up in these words, "Therefore, we conclude that a man is justified by faith without the deeds of the law" (Romans 3:28).

JAN.
19
Most of us stumble intellectually over the simplicity of the Gospel. We would like something complicated that would constitute a challenge to our intellects.

Certainly there are many things about Christianity that present a challenge to the greatest scholars, but when it comes to the way of salvation it is childlike in the best sense of the word. Jesus said, "Except ye be converted, and become as little children, ye shall not enter into the kingdom of heaven" (Matthew 18:3).

Perhaps you have never humbled yourself intellectually and entered the kingdom of God through the door of simple childlike faith in Christ. There is no other way and what a tragedy it would be if we were to let our intellectual pride keep us out of the presence of God.

JAN.
20
Christianity involves a choice. It is not the result of an educational process or a natural development. It is a spiritual transformation that takes place when we choose to commit our lives to God through faith in Christ.

When Moses came down from Mount Sinai and found the people worshiping the golden calf he called them together and demanded a decision in these words, "Who is on the Lord's side? Let him come unto me" (Exodus 32:26).

A few years later his successor did the same thing when he gave the Jewish people an opportunity to decide for God by saying, "Choose you this day whom ye will serve" (Joshua 24:15).

The Christian life is born when a man acts spiritually by accepting Christ. Jesus said, "Him that cometh unto me I will in no wise cast out" (John 6:37).

JAN. 21 The reason some people do not know God is that the eyes of their souls are blind and they cannot see the spiritual world.

We do not arrive at a knowledge of God through our physical faculties. Science and intellect do not show us God. He is known only through faith.

The Bible says, "The natural man receiveth not the things of the Spirit of God: for they are foolishness unto him: neither can he know them, because they are spiritually discerned" (I Corinthians 2:14).

The eyes of the soul are opened when we accept Christ as our Saviour and are born again.

JAN. 22 The Church is not the result of the organizational genius of man. Christ founded the Church and He builds the Church: "Upon this rock will I build my church: and the gates of hell shall not prevail against it" (Matthew 16:18).

It is difficult to understand how anyone could ignore the institution Christ inaugurated and expect to be right with God. The Church is not made up of isolated believers, but of a group "fitly framed together" (Ephesians 2:21) and founded upon Christ.

When a person receives the Lord and trusts Him as his Saviour there will be born within his heart a desire to have fellowship with others who have done the same thing. He will recognize that he is part of a huge temple that is being built by God and if it is physically possible he will seek out others who love the Lord and share his communion with the whole Church.

The Church is not a spiritual isolation ward — it is a divine assembly hall.

JAN. 23 The Bible calls for men and women who will take their stand for God. Sometimes this involves standing alone for something we believe in, and at best, it usually means standing with the minority, but this is the challenge of Jesus Christ.

Either we stand with Him and for Him, or we stand against Him and opposed to Him. Jesus said, "He that is not with me is against me" (Matthew 12:30).

The world needs men and women and boys and girls who will step out of the ranks of the crowd and stand for Christ.

JAN. 24 The person who does not know the Lord Jesus Christ is in the eternal quest for happiness, but it is always in the future.

He strives for it, but never realizes it. He reaches for it, but never grasps it. Happiness evades him at every turning. His ship never comes in. He looks forward to his retirement, when he thinks he can settle down and spend his wealth — only to find he is too old to enjoy it.

How different for the Christian! For him, happiness is always in the present. Joy comes in the moment he accepts Christ as his Saviour and continues throughout eternity.

The Bible says, "And whoso trusteth in the Lord, happy is he . . . Blessed is the man that walketh not in the counsel of the ungodly . . . At thy right hand there are pleasures for evermore" (Proverbs 16:20; Psalms 1:1; 16:11).

JAN. 25

It is essential to have had a real experience with God through faith in Christ. However, this experience means little if it is not demonstrated in a Christian life that is characterized by reality.

Jesus said, "I am the light of the world: he that followeth me shall not walk in darkness, but shall have the light of life" (John 8:12).

The world can only see the light that shines, the power that acts, and the faith that works. There must be reality in our Christian experience. Without it we are lost. There must be reality in our Christian living. Without this our friends may be lost.

JAN. 26

Many people expect to enter heaven by way of the Christian religion and among the great religions, Christianity is the greatest. However, we should realize that the religion of Christ cannot take us to heaven. It is Christ Himself who has the power to save.

It is possible to be an adherent of the Christian religion without being in personal contact with the Christ of Christianity. "It is Christ that died, yea rather, that is risen again, who is even at the right hand of God, who also maketh intercession for us" (Romans 8:34).

He is the only saving link between man and God. He is the Mediator, the Intercessor, the Saviour. The Christian religion is not the way to God. Jesus Christ alone has the power to re-unite a fallen man with a holy God.

JAN. 27   Jesus pictured the world in terms of a farmer's field in which wheat and weeds are growing side by side.

The wheat represents the children of God and the tares represent the children of the devil.

The farmer in the story said, "Let both grow together until the harvest: and in the time of harvest I will say to the reapers, Gather ye together first the tares, and bind them in bundles to burn them: but gather the wheat into my barn" (Matthew 13:30).

God sees all of us as wheat or weeds, depending upon our relationship to Jesus Christ. It is vital that we know Christ and be numbered with the wheat.

JAN. 28   Superman can do anything, but then Superman is just a cartoon, the figment of an artist's imagination.

The rest of us do not live long before we realize that we need one another. We are dependent upon other people, but more important than this, we are dependent upon God.

The Bible says, "He that trusteth in his own heart is a fool," but the Bible also says, "I can do all things through Christ which strengtheneth me" (Proverbs 28:26; Philippians 4:13).

Try to cut out a corner of the world for yourself and by yourself and you will be a failure. Trust Jesus Christ as your Saviour and you become a child of God with all of the resources of heaven at your disposal.

JAN. 29 No home is really Christian until the wall of salvation has been built. This means that every member of the family must be saved.

A father who has never trusted Christ as his Saviour prevents his home from being Christian. A mother who is not right with God makes it impossible for her home to be Christian. A son or daughter who has never been saved hinders that home from being Christian.

The Apostle Paul urged the Philippian jailer, "Believe on the Lord Jesus Christ and thou shalt be saved, and thy house" (Acts 16:31). The man believed and was saved. His family believed and they were saved, and the wall of salvation was completed to form another Christian home.

JAN. 30 Jesus was able to turn a milling mob of bewildered people into an orderly group when He fed the five thousand in the wilderness.

They were men and women without a purpose, caught in the vicious circle of working to maintain their existence. They had no objective in life, no goal, no focal point.

This is typical of the majority of people today. Life is a continuous round of the same things. There seems little to live for.

The Apostle Paul found a spiritual focal point, a reason for being alive, when he trusted Jesus Christ as his Saviour. Instead of merely existing, he was able to say, "I am crucified with Christ: nevertheless I live; yet not I, but Christ liveth in me: and the life which I now live in the flesh, I live by the faith of the Son of God . . . For me to live is Christ" (Galatians 2:20; Philippians 1:21).

JAN.
31 Every Christian should be a member of some church, but being a church member does not make a man a Christian.

Many people believe that church membership is the doorway to heaven, but Jesus said, "I am the door: by me if any man enter in, he shall be saved" (John 10:9).

It is possible to join the church and not know Jesus Christ as a personal Saviour. The church is needed, but salvation comes when we give our lives to God and trust His Son as our Saviour.

FEB.
1
The Bible presents a dual motivation to God. No one could read the inspired words without sensing the compelling power of love. Nor is it possible to go far through its pages without being alerted to the urgent note of fear that is struck.

"Yea, I have loved thee with an everlasting love: therefore with lovingkindness have I drawn thee" (Jeremiah 31:3). Usually, the Old Testament is associated with the vengeance of God, but of course, every student of the Bible knows that love is by no means foreign to the pages of the Old Testament.

Jesus emphasized the necessity of fear many times. For example, He once said, "Fear him which is able to destroy both soul and body in hell" (Matthew 10:28).

Some are driven by fear and others are drawn by love. Most people are moved by a combination of both. It is not important to know the motivating power, but it is eternally imperative that some force either pulls or pushes us to God.

FEB.
2
It is impossible to prove scientifically that God exists. No one has ever done it. No one will ever do it in the future.

The methods of science have done wonders in the material world, but they are powerless to touch the spiritual world. The Bible makes it clear that faith is the door that leads man into the presence of God and that without faith it is impossible to please God or know God.

"But without faith it is impossible to please him: For he that cometh to God must believe that he is, and that he is a rewarder of them that diligently seek him" (Hebrews 11:6).

Science has never proved nor disproved the Christian hope and it never will, but the Bible says, "Therefore being justified by faith, we have peace with God through our Lord Jesus Christ" (Romans 5:1).

FEB.
3
There are hundreds of intelligent people who think that the most God can expect of any man is that he do the best he can. However, the Bible declares that our best is not good enough. "There is none that doeth good, no not one. All our righteousnesses are as filthy rags" (Romans 3:12; Isaiah 64:6).

If we are to be saved, we must trust Christ and thus share in His righteousness. That is why the Apostle Paul said, "But of him are ye in Christ Jesus, who of God is made unto us wisdom, and righteousness, and sanctification, and redemption" (I Corinthians 1:30).

Our best always falls short of the mark. It may be better than the best of others, but it is still less than God requires. When we accept Christ, God performs a miracle that clothes us in the righteousness of Jesus. "He hath made us accepted in the beloved" (Colossians 1:6).

FEB.
4
Someday I will die. Death could be sudden and unheralded or it could be lingering and well publicized. At the time of my death, I may have a large bank account, a paid-off mortgage on my home, an educated family and a fair reputation.

But when I die, as far as I am concerned personally, my greatest anxiety will be about my future. The material existence of the past I must leave. The spiritual reality of eternity I must face.

God called one man a fool because he was not ready for death. "Thou fool, this night thy soul shall be required of thee: then whose shall those things be, which thou hast provided?" (Luke 12:20).

FEB.
5

Nearly two thousand years ago Jesus Christ said, "Come unto me, all ye that labour and are heavy laden, and I will give you rest" (Matthew 11:28).

The majority of people are carrying heavy burdens. As a matter of fact, many of our activities constitute attempts to unload some of the weight of living in a world where a sort of gravity that has nothing to do with physical objects seems to drag us down and prevent our natural desire to soar into the heavenlies. Most of us have tried just about everything — friends, family, work, entertainment, maybe even some kind of religion, but sometimes we trudge along for years without trying God's answer — Jesus Christ.

May I suggest that you commit your life to Him right now? Let Him begin to help you bear your burdens and change the whole course of your life.

FEB.
6

Some people are not Christians — because they are too busy! This is an active world. Civilization is going places and most of us are almost out of breath in our attempt to keep up the pace.

In this kind of a world, it is easy to become so engaged in the activities of living that we do not take time to prepare for the business of dying.

Take a moment to think. You are a soul and you need to be fed spiritually. You are moving toward death and you must be ready for it. Beyond death is the judgment and you must face it.

The Bible says, "For whosoever shall call upon the name of the Lord shall be saved" (Romans 10:13). It takes but a moment of your busy schedule to call, but the result will last forever. Do not be too busy to feed your soul and get right with God.

FEB. 7

Most people think that they have managed to hide their sin successfully. The criminal lives under the assumption that he can commit the perfect crime, but people who are authorities say that there is no such thing as a perfect crime. Somewhere a mistake is made, regardless of the amount of careful planning that may have been done.

Because "men loved darkness rather than light" (John 3:19), they have tried for centuries to commit the perfect sin. But the Bible declares that there is no perfect sin. "Be sure your sin will find you out" (Numbers 32:23).

Sin will be exposed in this world or the next. Happy is the man whose sin finds him out in this world and he lives to experience repentance and confession and reunion with God. Wretched is the man who hides his sin in this world and has to stand before God at the judgment and see his sin exposed after it is too late to do anything about it.

FEB. 8

There are many people who do not believe in God because they cannot prove anything about Him scientifically.

The Bible says, "What man knoweth the things of man, save the spirit of man which is in him? even so the things of God knoweth no man, but the Spirit of God" (I Corinthians 2:11).

Let me give you a suggestion that may help you to find God:

1) Begin to live as though there *is* a God.
2) Start to pray as though God *does* hear you.
3) Accept Christ as your Saviour and take it for granted that He *has* changed your life.

Do this for a few weeks, and you will discover that God is there, He does hear your prayer, and He has changed your life.

FEB.
9
"Without controversy great is the mystery of godliness" (I Timothy 3:16).

We have only to look back upon the remarkable elements that were drawn together to bring us to God and we find ourselves agreeing wholeheartedly with the great Apostle's statement. Usually it takes many people—a mother, a friend, a preacher. Sometimes there is a series of unique events and frequently there is the direct pressure of tragedy that finally enables us to hear the voice of God.

In the life of a Christian God often speaks through circumstances. The will of God is discovered by opened and closed doors. After we have turned away from the doors that are shut and walked by faith through those that are open, we say in retrospect, "The voice of God directed me."

Perhaps there are those who never hear the voice of God in their circumstances, but they can hear the call of God directly from His Word. Hear His urgent appeal to the unconverted. "The Lord thy God in the midst of thee is mighty; he will save, he will rejoice over thee with joy" (Zephaniah 3:17).

FEB.
10
Beyond this world of calloused hands and aching backs and frayed nerves and tense minds, there is a place called heaven. Jesus declared, "In my Father's house are many mansions: if it were not so, I would have told you. I go to prepare a place for you. And if I go and prepare a place for you, I will come again, and receive you unto myself; that where I am, there ye may be also" (John 14:2, 3).

Even the most stubborn rationalist needs a hope beyond this rather hopeless life that will make it all worthwhile. That hope is heaven and Jesus Christ is the only way to it. "He that spared not his own Son, but delivered him up for us all, how shall he not with him also freely give us all things?" (Romans 8:32).

FEB. 11   The civilization of this world is characterized by favoritism. The rich man can often buy another chance and the poor man can sometimes beg one. The artist and the musician are excused because they are temperamental. The educated man can devise his escape from justice and the illiterate may plead his ignorance.

In God's books there is no distinction. Judgment is on the basis of sin and there are no favorites. The Bible states that "God is no respecter of persons . . . for there is no difference: For all have sinned, and come short of the glory of God" (Acts 10:34; Romans 3:22-23).

That is why everyone, regardless of his station in life, must come to God through faith in Christ and be saved.

FEB. 12   It is possible for us to know a person who does not know us. I can truthfully say that I know the Queen of England. I know who she is. I know where she lives. I know something about her family, but the Queen does not know me. This is what we usually mean when we use the word "know" in connection with famous people. We know them but they do not know us.

This is not what the Bible means when it talks about knowing God. It is not a long distance, one-way relationship with God; but that is all many people have; they know God in the sense that they recognize His existence and perhaps His power, but God does not admit any connection. About a group of people who thought they should enter heaven Jesus said, "Then will I profess unto them, I never knew you" (Matthew 7:23).

A long distance, one-way relationship with God is not Christianity.

FEB.
13
There are many rich men who would give away their entire fortunes, if someone could assure them of ten more years of life. But even the medical profession cannot sell life.

When death lays its hand upon an individual, he must go, and all the science in the world cannot detain him.

We cannot buy life, but we can have it for nothing. When we trust Jesus Christ as our Saviour, He brings eternal life with him. "And this is the record, that God hath given to us eternal life, and this life is in His Son" (I John 5:11).

This was the promise of Christ: "I am come that they might have life, and that they might have it more abundantly" (John 10:10).

FEB.
14
Christianity involves an immediate choice. Hundreds of years ago an old man addressed a huge crowd and said, "Choose you this day whom you will serve" (Joshua 24:15).

He said "this day" because he knew that for some of those people there would never be another day. This shortness of time is true in a sense for all of us. The only time that belongs to us is now. Tomorrow is in the hands of God. Today we can make decisions. Tomorrow that privilege may be gone.

That is why the Bible says, "Behold, now is the day of salvation . . . Boast not thyself of tomorrow; for thou knowest not what a day may bring forth" (II Corinthians 6:2; Proverbs 27:1).

You may have many years ahead of you, but no one can be sure of the next twenty-four hours. The wise man takes advantage of the immediate present — the now of life that is his.

FEB.
15
Perhaps the deepest longing of the human heart is to love and to be loved. The most wretched man on earth is the man who has no one to love. The loneliest man in the world is the person who is loved by no one.

Love is one of the intangible values in human life that is not for sale on the markets of the world. We can buy time and talent and work and even obedience, but we cannot buy love.

To those who have never known the meaning of real love in the highest sense of the term, the Bible speaks with a message of encouragement, "Herein is love, not that we loved God, but that he loved us, and sent his Son to be the propitiation for our sins" (I John 4:10).

FEB.
16
Nobody ever "makes it" to heaven. Only the power of God, the mercy of God, and the grace of God open the door and carry the sinner in.

Many a man goes through life trying to offset the bad by the good and as he approaches the end of the road he thinks, *I believe I've made it.* The tragedy is that he has not made it. Philanthropist and humanitarian though he may have been, he has not made it, because the Bible declares that all men fall short of the mark.

The Apostle Peter reminds us that to some extent God must even judge the Christian, and if so, what possible chance has the one who is not a Christian? "The time is come that judgment must begin at the house of God: and if it first begin at us, what shall the end be of them that obey not the gospel of God?" (I Peter 4:17).

Oh, that we would make sure that our good works have as their foundation a personal experience with the Son of God who has saved us from our sins! Otherwise we are lost.

FEB. 17

It is a sad affair to go through life alone. To face the problems without help, to bear the diseases and frailties of the body without comfort, and to be driven toward the darkness of death without a friend, is indeed a difficult lot. Most people do this very thing because in these areas of life even the dearest of human friends falls short of our need.

The disciples sensed this loneliness when they faced death in a storm at sea. Although they had one another, they were alone in their need. It was not until Jesus came walking to them on the water that they felt the companionship that they so desperately needed.

In our hour of need today, the same words that brought blessing to these men can bring help to us, "Be of good cheer; it is I; be not afraid" (Matthew 14:27).

FEB. 18

Sometimes we measure a man's intelligence by his farsightedness. The quarterback on a football team who can think ahead of the play he is calling, the checker player who plans three moves while he is making one, the business man who can see beyond today's bargain counters — by worldly standards, these are wise men.

According to the Bible, you and I must live somewhere forever. Beyond the realm of space and time there is everlasting punishment and everlasting life.

In view of this fact — by the world's standards — how intelligent are you? Have you been farsighted enough to plan for your eternity?

The Bible says, "For he that soweth to his flesh shall of the flesh reap corruption; but he that soweth to the Spirit shall of the Spirit reap life everlasting" (Galatians 6:8).

FEB. 19 There are four sides to everyone's life — the physical, the mental, the recreational, and the spiritual. If we neglect any one of these, we become lopsided people.

Perhaps you have looked after every other part of your life, but you have let your spiritual life suffer. In this material-mad world many people have done that and scores of them are on the verge of a mental break-down.

The Bible says, "Trust in the Lord and do good . . . Delight thyself also in the Lord; and he shall give thee the desires of thine heart. Commit thy way unto the Lord; trust also in him; and he shall bring it to pass" (Psalm 37:3-5).

FEB. 20 Man's sense of justice demands a day of reckoning. There is a ghastly deficiency in moral balance in the world.

The drunkard thrives, the harlot is secure, the blasphemer prospers, the murderer goes unpunished, the liar is exonerated, the thief lives in luxury, and the degenerate lives and dies in peace. In the face of the filthy facts of modern civilization our sense of moral equality cries out that sin someday must be punished, wrong somehow must be righted, and justice somewhere must be done.

It is not a surprise to anyone to find the principle of judgment throughout the entire Bible. "They that plough iniquity, and sow wickedness, reap the same. For they have sown the wind, and they shall reap the whirlwind" (Job 4:8, Hosea 8:7).

It is a fortunate man who is convicted of his sin and gets right with God through faith in Christ. It is pitiful for a man to reject the offer of mercy now and reap the whirlwind later.

FEB. 21 "How hardly shall they that have riches enter into the kingdom of God" (Luke 18:24).

Hardly, because material prosperity makes it difficult to realize spiritual poverty.

Perhaps it is more difficult for a good man to be saved. He is so blinded by his self-righteousness and human morality that he cannot see his sinfulness.

Jesus said, "For I am not come to call the righteous, but sinners to repentance" (Matthew 9:13). Admission of sin is the first step toward salvation and it is repulsive for a man who is good in the eyes of the world to confess that he is a sinner in the eyes of God.

No one will take the step of faith that results in salvation until he has been stripped of his human righteousness and comes before God as a sinner.

FEB. 22 It is possible to be converted and not be re-generated.

Conversion is something that we can accomplish ourselves. We can be converted to a church, a preacher, a mother or a sweetheart. These can bring a pressure to bear that causes us to turn and go the other way.

Regeneration is a miracle that only God can perform. We are born into the family of God when we become so convicted of our sin that we seek salvation through faith in Christ.

The Bible says, "But as many as received him, to them gave he power to become the sons of God, even to them that believe on his name. Which were born, not of blood, nor of the will of the flesh, nor of the will of man, but of God" (John 1:12-13).

FEB.
23
The Bible assumes that some men have heard the voice of God audibly. Our first parents "heard the voice of the Lord God walking in the garden in the cool of the day" (Genesis 3:8).

Elijah expected to hear from God through a wind, then an earthquake, and finally a fire. None of these spoke to him, but after these had come and gone the Bible says he heard "a still small voice" (I Kings 19:2).

On the Damascus road the Apostle Paul "heard a voice saying unto him, Saul, Saul, why persecutest thou me?" (Acts 9:4).

We may never hear the voice of God speaking to us audibly as these people did, but we have within our hands and in our hearts the inspired Word of God which speaks to us as God did to Adam and Eve or Elijah or Paul.

Hear the voice of God to the condemned sinner: "There is therefore now no condemnation to them which are in Christ Jesus, who walk not after the flesh but after the Spirit" (Romans 8:1).

FEB.
24
The tragedy of maturity in physical life is that we tend to lose the wonder and warmth of living. Happy is the man who can keep the flame of interest and intensity in life burning.

Jesus condemned the church of Ephesus because the glow of spiritual glory had become dim there. The fire of Christian fervor had almost died out. In spite of the good orthodox reputation of the church, Jesus said, "Nevertheless I have somewhat against thee, because thou hast left thy first love" (Revelation 2:4).

It is a spiritual tragedy when a Christian loses the wonder and warmth of his first love for his Lord.

FEB. 25 One of the obvious characteristics of a baby is immaturity. He has the full potential of a man but he is not a man. He is born at a given moment but it takes years for him to become a man.

Spiritual life starts the moment a man trusts Christ as his Saviour, but it takes months and sometimes years for him to develop into a mature Christian. While he is young in the faith, he may stumble and fall and make mistakes, but realizing that he is immature and must grow, he confesses his failure to God, gets up on his spiritual feet, and goes on living for God.

The Bible says that we must "all come in the unity of the faith, and of the knowledge of the Son of God, unto a perfect man, unto the measure of the stature of the fulness of Christ" (Ephesians 4:13).

FEB. 26 The Lord Jesus Christ changed the entire course of the lives of eleven men one day when He said, "Let not your heart be troubled" (John 14:27).

It is possible to live in a world of war and have a heart that is not troubled. You may live in a city filled with strife and have a heart that is not troubled. You may even live right in a home that is in a state of constant uproar and strife and have a heart that is free from trouble.

When we trust Jesus Christ as our personal Saviour He gives us eternal life and makes us the children of God, but He also puts within our hearts His peace — the peace that passeth understanding. No matter what the conditions may be on the outside He keeps our hearts in perfect peace because they are stayed upon Him.

FEB. 27   The best test of Christianity is sin. The Apostle John says, "We know that whosoever is born of God sinneth not" (I John 5:18).

Any Christian may slip and fall spiritually, but he does not do it deliberately and continually. It is possible for a Christian to lie, to be jealous, to lose his temper, but if a man continues to do these things without any regrets or shame, he is obviously not a child of God.

FEB. 28   Some day we must all give an account of ourselves unto God. Most of us could give a fine account of our acquaintances. We know the shortcomings of the other members of the family. We have seen the apparent worldliness of our neighbors. We are conversant about the faults of the preacher and we could talk indefinitely about the hypocrites in the church.

However, on the day of judgment we will not be required to account for the deeds of anyone else. We will stand alone before God, "The son shall not bear the iniquity of the father, neither shall the father bear the iniquity of the son: the righteousness of the righteous shall be upon him, and the wickedness of the wicked shall be upon him" (Ezekiel 18:20).

FEB. 29   The written word reaches vast audiences but on a personal level. It does its work in the privacy of a heathen hut, in the loneliness of a trapper's tent, or in the isolation of a convict's cell. It blesses the sailor far from home, guides the soldier overseas, and comforts the invalid who cannot go to church. It enables a man to closet himself in the sanctuary of his heart and to hear God's voice.

"The word of God is quick, and powerful, and sharper than any two-edged sword, and is a discerner of the thoughts and intents of the heart" (Hebrews 4:12). The man who neglects the Bible neglects the only Book in which God speaks to him directly.

MARCH 1

There are three transactions which produce a Christian. The first involves committal to the Messiah. The Bible says: "Whosoever believeth that Jesus is the Christ is born of God" (I John 5:1).

Then follows cleansing in the blood of Christ. The Bible says: "Jesus Christ . . . that loved us, and washed us from our sins in his own blood" (Revelation 1:5).

The third element is regeneration. The Bible speaks about: "Being born again, not of corruptible seed, but of incorruptible, by the word of God" (I Peter 1:23).

The first transaction is in the hands of man. He may trust or not trust as he chooses. The other two are miracles that must be performed by God. How the blood of Christ cleanses us from our sins is a wonder beyond our comprehension. How a man can be reborn so that he lives forever is a miracle that overwhelms us but this is the truth of the Gospel. We commit our lives in faith to Christ and God cleanses us from sin and converts us into sons in the divine family.

MARCH 2

Jesus told a story about five foolish young women who missed the most important appointment of their lives because they were not prepared for it.

They intended to go, and they expected to get in, but the Bible says they were shut out because they had failed to buy oil for their lamps. "And while they went to buy, the bridegroom came; and they that were ready went in with him to the marriage: and the door was shut" (Matthew 25:10).

Most people expect to go to heaven but have not made the necessary preparation by doing whatever is necessary to get right with God.

MARCH 3   Religion is a good thing and everyone has some kind of religion, but the Bible makes it clear that religion will not save us spiritually or make us the children of God. Not even the Christian religion can do that.

Personal salvation comes as a result of your relation — not to a religion — but to a Person. You must commit your life by faith to Jesus Christ, God's Son. The Bible says, "Neither is there salvation in any other" (Acts 4:12). Jesus said, "I am the way . . . no man cometh unto the Father, but by me" (John 14:6).

You may have some kind of religion but what you really need is a Saviour.

MARCH 4   It is possible to be prepared for this world and not be prepared for the next — to be geared for time but not for eternity.

The Bible makes it apparent that the years of this life are but a shadow compared to the vast scope of the next. "My days are swifter than a weaver's shuttle, and are spent without hope. . . . For what is your life? It is even a vapour, that appeareth for a little time, and then vanisheth away" (Job 7:6; James 4:14).

Jesus urged His disciples to concentrate upon building up a spiritual bank account in heaven: "Lay not up for yourselves treasures upon earth, where moth and dust doth corrupt and where thieves break through and steal: But lay up for yourselves treasures in heaven, where neither moth nor rust doth corrupt and where thieves do not break through nor steal: For where your treasure is, there will your heart be also" (Matthew 6:19-21).

MARCH 5 Throughout all of the Scriptures man is represented as lost. He is lost in the sense that his sinfulness has separated him from God and he cannot find his way back to God.

The religions of man are his attempts to find God but the Bible declares that the ways to God that would seem right to man are usually wrong. The Old Testament says, "There is a way that seemeth right unto a man, but the end thereof are the ways of death" (Proverbs 14:12).

In the New Testament Jesus clarifies the issue by pointing to Himself and saying, "I am the way . . . no man cometh unto the Father, but by me" (John 14:6).

Man is lost until he finds his way back to God through faith in Christ.

MARCH 6 There are many people who read the Bible regularly and know a considerable amount about it but they have never accepted Christ as their Saviour and do not know what it means to be born into the family of God.

James likens this kind of person to a man who looks into the mirror, sees a defect of some sort, and goes away without correcting it. "Be ye doers of the word, and not hearers only . . . For if any be a hearer of the word, and not a doer, he is like unto a man beholding his natural face in a glass: For he beholdeth himself, and goeth his way, and straightway forgetteth what manner of man he was" (James 1:22-24).

If the mirror of God's Word tells me there is a moral smudge on my life, an ethical stain in my character, or some business dirt in my conduct, I must do something about it, by getting right with God.

MARCH 7 God gives every man the choice of accepting the wages he has earned by his sinning or the gift Jesus Christ purchased for him by His death on the cross.

If the gift is not accepted the wages must be paid. The Bible depicts man as being in a position where he is free to choose. When he refuses to yield his life to God and continues to live in sin, he is daily earning the wages that sin always pays. When he trusts Jesus Christ as his Saviour, he receives the gift of God.

The Bible says, "For the wages of sin is death; but the gift of God is eternal life through Jesus Christ our Lord" (Romans 6:23).

MARCH 8 The majority of the people we know are little more than casual acquaintances. We have been introduced and we have spent some time with them. There has been a mutual exchange of names and ideas and time. These are our friends. We know them casually.

This does not describe what the Bible means when it says we can know God. However, this is all most people have — a casual relationship with Jesus Christ. Usually it involves a certain building at a specified hour on a particular day when a man "pays his respects" to Jesus Christ by going to church. During the rest of the week he lives as if God were dead.

Jesus spoke of this kind of person when He said: "This people honoureth me with their lips, but their heart is far from me" (Mark 7:6). Ezekiel uncovered the same thing: "They come unto thee as the people cometh, and they sit before me as my people, and they hear thy words, but they will not do them" (Ezekiel 33:31).

**MARCH
9**
Probably the greatest single indication of strong human love is the desire to serve the one we love.

When Saul of Tarsus met Jesus Christ on the Damascus road and was converted, his first reaction was to ask, "Lord, what wilt thou have me to do?" (Acts 9:6).

Love is demonstrated by service and when the urge to be active in the work of God is gone, we need revival.

Even as an old man with years of service behind him, Joshua was able to say, "But as for me and my house, we will serve the Lord" (Joshua 24:15).

**MARCH
10**
Archaeology has added much to the authority of the Bible. The more scientists can uncover the past, the more the teaching of the Bible is confirmed. Research does not shake our confidence in the written Word; it establishes it.

However, the Christian does not accept the Bible because science proves it. He accepts it on the rock of intelligent faith and watches patiently as research brings science closer and closer to the truth of the inspired Book.

Archaeological investigation may eventually confirm the story of Genesis but the child of God knows through faith that the creation account is exactly as it happened. "Through faith we understand that the worlds were framed by the word of God, so that things which are seen were not made of things that do appear" (Hebrews 11:3).

When a person trusts Christ and believes the Bible, he is accepting by faith what may be the facts of science a thousand years from now.

MARCH 11   Luke's rich farmer was obviously an industrious man, but Jesus referred to him as a fool.

He was not foolish because he was industrious. The Bible commends hard work. God ordained that man should work by the sweat of his brow. Proverbs says, "Go to the ant, thou sluggard; consider her ways, and be wise" (Proverbs 6:6).

This man had allowed his intense activity to cloud his relationship to God. He was extremely busy — so busy that he had no time for God, and for this Jesus condemned him as a fool.

It is essential that each individual make time to meet God and take time to commit his life to Him.

MARCH 12   Do you realize that it is impossible for us to be neutral in our attitudes toward Jesus Christ? When we hear about Him we must either accept or reject Him.

If we have never accepted Him, by the cold conclusion of logic, we have automatically rejected Him. One of the dictionary definitions of the word "reject" is "failure to accept."

The Bible says, "But as many as received him, to them gave he power to become the sons of God, even to them that believe on his name" (John 1:12).

It is one thing to hear about Christ and to have the way of salvation explained. It is quite another thing to respond to the message and accept Jesus Christ. The first results in intellectual enlightenment. The second brings us to God.

MARCH 13 According to the Bible a Christian and a non-Christian can never enjoy real fellowship in their married life until both have been saved.

When a Christian girl deliberately marries a boy who is not saved, or vice versa, she is asking for tragedy in one of the most important relationships of her life.

The Apostle Paul warned, "Be ye not unequally yoked together with unbelievers: for what fellowship hath righteousness with unrighteousness? and what communion hath light with darkness?" (II Corinthians 6:14).

This principle is not only good theology, it is good psychology. There is no more ruthless, dogmatic, emotional, and intense area of life than the realm of religion. Two opposing religious beliefs have no more hope of surviving properly in the same house than has light and darkness.

MARCH 14 The farmer in the story narrated in Luke's gospel was rich, but Jesus described him as a fool.

I do not think it was his wealth that Jesus condemned. On one occasion He said, "How hard is it for them that trust in riches to enter into the kingdom of God" (Mark 10:24). However, nowhere did Jesus say that to enter is impossible.

Obviously, material prosperity makes it difficult to appreciate spiritual poverty, but it is only when the almighty dollar takes the place of Almighty God that riches become an obstacle to heaven.

Giving away material possessions does not open the door to heaven, but trusting Christ as Saviour and following Him as Lord does.

MARCH 15 Man is pictured in three different conditions in the Bible: 1) In the Garden — walking with God, innocent and purely sinless; 2) after the fall — with no fellowship with God and the Divine Image marred by sin; 3) redeemed by grace — the righteousness of God Himself imputed to sinful man through faith in Jesus Christ.

The Bible is consistent in stating that all have sinned, "The good man is perished out of the earth: and there is none upright among men" (Micah 7:2), but it is equally consistent in affirming that all can be "justified freely by his grace through the redemption that is in Christ Jesus" (Romans 3:24.)

Sin is a universal fact.

Salvation is a universal possibility.

But the response of man to the provision of God is a personal matter. Man can accept it or reject it.

MARCH 16 Christianity is more than a philosophy of life or a system of religion. It is a personal experience with Jesus Christ that enables a man to know God and be alert to the voice of God.

Jesus referred to Himself as the Good Shepherd and He promised that His sheep would know His voice and would follow Him. "And when he putteth forth his own sheep, he goeth before them, and the sheep follow him: for they know his voice" (John 10:4).

It is possible to attend church but not know the voice of God. The Christian attends the House of God, but also he has had a spiritual experience with Jesus Christ that has put him into direct contact with God.

MARCH 17 Some people object to the idea that God would condemn anyone, but think that because of His love and mercy, He will save all men.

Certainly God does not desire the wicked to be lost. The Bible says that God is "not willing that any should perish, but that all should come to repentance. . . As I live, saith the Lord God, I have no pleasure in the death of the wicked; but that the wicked turn from his way and live" (II Peter 3:9, Ezekiel 33:11).

Salvation has been provided, but man must reach out with the arm of faith and take it.

MARCH 18 Privilege and participation are two different things.

Theoretically, any boy born in the United States has the privilege of becoming the President. However, participation in this privilege is determined by entry into and success in politics. Thousands of American-born boys never even take the first step that could lead to participation in the privilege of the chief executive.

Paul must have been blessed when he was able to write, "All things work together for good." He was stating one of the privileges of man — to live a life in which the best and the worst things result in good things.

The Apostle is quick to add the conditions of participation in this privilege, "to them that love God, to them who are called according to his purpose" (Romans 8:28). It is our love for God and obedience to His purpose that pave the way for us to participate in this miraculous privilege.

MARCH 19 Is a man who breaks the law a sick person whose case needs diagnosis and treatment or is he a sinner who should be punished? This is the basic problem that we are reading about today in the heated discussion over the abolition of capital punishment.

The Bible makes it clear that we are free moral agents. We know what is right and what is wrong. We can do what is right or we can do what is wrong. If we choose to do wrong and break the moral law, we are in line to be punished. Apart from a small percentage of mentally deficient exceptions to this rule, the law applies to every normal individual regardless of good or bad environment.

The New Testament declares that "Whatsoever a man soweth, that shall he also reap" (Galatians 6:7).

MARCH 20 Christianity is a paradox to the human mind. Some of the basic principles that Jesus taught are not only difficult to understand, but they seem rather ludicrous.

God had to perform a mircle in the minds of the disciples before they could accept the fact that greatness in the language of heaven is described in terms of service. In the Kingdom of God, greatness is not determined by wealth or position or ability. It is seen and estimated in degrees of humility.

When James and John asked Jesus for positions of honor in the Kingdom, He answered, "But whosoever will be great among you, shall be your minister. And whosoever of you shall be the chiefest, shall be servant of all" (Mark 10:43-44).

No one can live in accordance with this principle until he has been born again and his thinking processes have been straightened out by God.

MARCH 21 Real forgiveness is almost completely foreign in human relations. Wherever there is deep-seated enmity between two groups or two individuals it is seldom forgotten. The Moslems cannot forgive the Christians. The Jews have never forgiven the Arabs and perhaps the United States will never forgive Cuba.

The message of the Bible could well be captioned the "Gospel of Forgiveness." "Be it known unto you therefore, men and brethren, that through this man is preached unto you the forgiveness of sins" (Acts 13:38). Unconditional surrender of our lives to Christ results in unconditional forgiveness of our sins from God.

Evidence of the forgiveness that we have experienced is our ability to put into practice the seemingly impossible admonition of the Master to Peter when he asked, "How oft shall my brother sin against me, and I forgive him? till seven times?

"Jesus saith unto him, I say not unto thee, Until seven times: but until seventy times seven" (Matthew 18:21:22).

MARCH 22 Perhaps the greatest weakness in our modern Christian churches can best be described by the word "nominalism." Many people are Christians on the outside. They are covered with the veneer of Christian civilization.

The Bible makes it clear that real Christianity begins on the inside with a complete spiritual revolution. Jesus said, "Marvel not that I said unto thee, Ye must be born again" (John 3:7).

This revolution takes place when we commit our lives to God through faith in Christ. This is a real experience that gives our faith the character of reality rather than superficiality.

MARCH 23 It is a wonderful thing to accept Jesus Christ as our Saviour. It is a much better thing to let the world know we have done so.

You will find it difficult to be a secret believer. You will gain spiritual strength when you declare yourself publicly.

Jesus said, "Whosoever therefore shall confess me before men, him will I confess also before my Father which is in heaven" (Matthew 10:32).

If you have accepted the Light of the Gospel, do not "put it under a bushel, but on a candlestick; and it giveth light unto all that are in the house" (Matthew 5:15).

MARCH 24 There are three courts of authority to which modern man may appeal. The first is tradition, but this may involve doctrines that were unheard of in the Christian Church for half a millenium — such as the Assumption of the Virgin Mary. This doctrine may be quite innocent and harmless, but wrong as a requirement of faith.

The second is reason and, although it is extremely valuable, it is by no means infallible. There was a time when reason told us the world was flat, that the atom was indivisible, and that the sun circumnavigated this world.

The third is the Bible. Apart from a paragraph in Josephus and a few lines in Tacitus, the only historical record we have of the life and ministry of Jesus is in the Bible. If we would be Christians we are left with one supreme court of appeal — the written Word of God.

The Bible says, "God hath not appointed us to wrath, but to obtain salvation by our Lord Jesus Christ, who died for us, that, whether we wake or sleep, we should live together with him" (I Thessalonians 5:9-10).

MARCH 25 The Bible contains the answers to all of the major problems of life. The tragedy of the average Christian's experience is that he goes everywhere else first and to the Bible only as a last resort.

After he has made an irreparable mess of his life as a result of following the advice of man, the Christian makes his way to his pastor's study and his attention is turned to the only absolute voice of authority — the Word of God. Then he gets his answer, but unfortunately it is usually too late.

The Psalmist said, "Before I was afflicted, I went astray: but now have I kept thy word. Thou art good, and doest good; teach me thy statutes" (Psalm 119:67, 68).

MARCH 26 Religious activity can never be a substitute for Christ. The thirst of the human heart cannot be satisfied by a build-up of good deeds, or a series of humanitarian donations, or a period of intense religious therapy.

These are all good things but without Jesus Christ who is the Water of Life they are like Jeremiah's "cisterns, broken cisterns, that can hold no water" (Jeremiah 2:13).

The woman with whom the Lord talked at the well was spiritually thirsty. Jesus did not advise her to go back to town and become active in some religious organization. He knew that mere religious activity would still leave her dry.

He urged her to find in a personal commitment to Him a spring of living water that would quench her thirst forever. "If thou knewest the gift of God thou wouldest have asked of him, and he would have given thee living water" (John 4:10).

MARCH 27 Sin seldom appears naked. The devil usually dresses it up so that it looks glamorous or successful, or popular, or romantic.

When a man is tempted to steal or murder he does not see the arm of the law that will bring him before a jury that will sentence him to prison or to the electric chair. What he does see is the money and what it will buy and where it will take him and the power it will give him.

The Bible is the book that uncovers sin and describes it in its naked form with all of its terrible penalties. The Bible warns us of the final destiny and reward of all sin, "Sin, when it is finished, bringeth forth death" (James 1:15).

MARCH 28 Christianity in these 1960's has become rather popular. We can boast of more members, more impressive ecclesiastical machinery, higher budgets, superior equipment, and better techniques than at any time in church history, but in some cases we have lost sight of the Lord.

We are like the people of Jeremiah's day about whom he lamented, "Though they say, The Lord liveth; surely they swear falsely" (Jeremiah 5:2). These people had a well-organized religious system but little real spirituality, so that heathen peoples might well look at their religion and then ask, "Where is their God?"

It is true that Jesus Christ is at the heart of many of today's religious organizations. He is often central in the use of modern techniques and may be foremost in the programs of churches with large memberships. However, it is quite possible to have all these outward manifestations of spiritual success and lack the pre-eminence of the Saviour that puts life and purpose into them.

It is a sad thing when an organization says: The Lord liveth and swears falsely. It can be eternally irreparable if this is true of an individual.

MARCH 29 Everything that man has ever laid his hand upon will finally change and pass away. Whether a sound be harmonious or discordant it will end. The most fragrant scent will drift away. The sharpest taste will become flat and be lost. Even the rocks are continually crumbling and changing.

The person who lives for these material and temporal things will eventually lose his world but the man who lives for God will find his world because he is in touch with the source from which all else came.

This is victory over the world and it is possible through faith in Christ. "Whosoever believeth that Jesus is the Christ is born of God: . . . For whatsoever is born of God overcometh the world: and this is the victory that overcometh the world, even our faith" (I John 5:1, 4).

MARCH 30 Christianity is not an idealogy to combat Communism, preserve a denomination, or crystallize an ethnic group.

Until the return in person of Jesus Christ there will always be some strong anti-god philosophy in the world whether it be Communism or something else. The rise and fall of any given denomination does not determine the strength of the Christian church, and the fact that a predominant number of people in a certain country call themselves Christians is not what ensures the existence of the Christian faith.

Christianity has to do with a personal relationship between a man and God that transcends human divisions and unites into one body all diverse elements, factions, and nationalities.

"For he is our peace, who hath made both one, and hath broken down the middle wall of partition between us" (Ephesians 2:14).

MARCH 31 When a Jew accepts Jesus Christ as his Messiah he does not cease to be a Jew. He changes his religion but he does not change his blood or his stomach. He may choose to eat kosher food for the rest of his life entirely apart from its religious significance.

This principle is true of any nationality or color or position in life. The miracle of the new birth is that God takes people who may be poles apart on the human level, and gives them a common spiritual denominator. He brings them to a point of union at which national, racial, and social distinctions are unimportant.

The Jew is still a Jew but in Christ he is a Christian. The Gentile maintains his characteristics but in Christ he is a Christian. The European remains a white man and the Indian a brown man but in Christ they are both Christians.

"There is neither Jew nor Greek, there is neither bond nor free, there is neither male nor female: for ye are all one in Christ" (Galatians 3:28).

Jesus Christ gives all of us — diverse though we may be — a common meeting ground.

APRIL 1

Many a book has been written on "The Quest for Happiness." And this is as it should be. Philosophers and educators and physicians have always recognized the need of man to be happy.

As a race we have sought happiness in many things and in many ways. We have tried learning and discipline and peace and war and love and money and friends and solitude and sometimes even a self-imposed poverty.

Most of us would work for anything that would produce happiness and we would sacrifice anything if it would result in happiness.

The Bible for many centuries has been patiently explaining that sin causes unhappiness and only the forgiveness of sin and a clear conscience before God produces happiness. Most of us feel that somehow we can find a way to circumvent the problem of sin and arrive at our happiness by some other route.

But the history of all of us writes an emphatic "Amen" across the pages of the Bible when it says, "Blessed is he whose transgression is forgiven, whose sin is covered" (Psalm 32:1).

APRIL 2

It is natural for young people to think they know all the answers and to conclude that their parents know little about modern living. However, the basic principles of life are learned not from books or school rooms, but from personal experience.

That is why the Bible says, "A fool despiseth his father's instruction: but he that regardeth reproof is prudent" (Proverbs 15:5).

The young person who has committed his life to God through faith in Christ is a Christian and a Christian respects the advice of the man or woman who has already been over the road, particularly if that person is also a Christian.

APRIL 3

If we are Christians, we have had a real spiritual experience with God through faith in Christ and the reality of our experience is being demonstrated in the reality of our Christian living. The reality of our Christian experience and the reality of our Christian lives may best be demonstrated by the reality of our Christian service.

Our Sunday school teaching and choir singing and organ playing and money giving and pulpit preaching may be nothing more than a part of the general veneer of our Christian civilization.

The Bible says, "Whatsoever thy hand findeth to do, do it with thy might" (Ecclesiastes 9:10). If we are aware of the seriousness of our Christian service, we will do this and our service to God will be as real as our experience with God.

APRIL 4

It is pointless to ask why man was created as he was with his various appetites and longings. The fact is that it is true.

We all have within us a yearning after spiritual satisfaction. The complete satisfaction of our physical appetites leaves us empty and bored and hungry. This is the sort of creatures we are.

It is to this spiritual vacuum in our human lives that the Bible appeals when it puts the message of the Gospel in terms of satisfaction. "Oh that men would praise the Lord for his goodness . . . For he satisfieth the longing soul, and filleth the hungry soul with goodness" (Psalm 107:8-9).

It is God that fills the life of man and we are empty until we find Him. The satiated material body will finally die and disappear, but the hungry spirit will last forever and unless it has been united with God through faith in Christ it will go on being empty forever.

APRIL 5   The Bible declares that there is an inbred tendency in man toward sin and until that tendency is completely changed by the power of God, no amount of good intentions or reformation will appreciably change a man's life.

David admitted this when he said, "Behold, I was shapen in iniquity; and in sin did my mother conceive me" (Psalm 51:5).

It is the heart of man that must be changed. His actions may be adjusted for a short time, but they will always revert to the original nature which is sinful.

The Bible says, "And I will give them one heart, and I will put a new spirit within you; and I will take the stony heart out of their flesh, and I will give them an heart of flesh" (Ezekiel 11:19).

APRIL 6   Sometimes a friend is better than a relative, and within the heart of man there is a longing for friendship. There is a sense in which any member of my family is a part of me, but a friend constitutes a source of support that is entirely outside of me.

The philosopher of the Old Testament said it this way, "Woe to him that is alone when he falleth; for he hath not another to help him up" (Ecclesiastes 4:10).

The Bible acknowledges this need in all of us when it depicts Jesus Christ, not only as a brother, but as a friend. "Greater love hath no man than this, that a man lay down his life for his friends. Ye are my friends, if ye do whatsoever I command you" (John 15:13-14).

Jesus offers us the gift of divine friendship, but with the reception of the gift He combines the responsibility of obedience to His commands.

We receive Christ by simple faith, but we also accept all that Christ involves. With the Divine Gift comes the Divine task.

APRIL 7   It is a serious mistake to talk maliciously about other people, but it is the easiest form of conversation and often the most interesting.

There are three questions that would prevent a great deal of slander and gossip. Before we speak critically, ask ourselves:

1) Is it true?
2) Is it kind?
3) Is it necessary?

The Bible says, "And he that uttereth a slander, is a fool" (Proverbs 10:18). Even when what we are about to relate is true God says, "Brethren, if a man be overtaken in a fault, ye which are spiritual restore such an one in the spirit of meekness; considering thyself, lest thou also be tempted" (Galatians 6:1).

Don't condemn him. Help him back to God.

APRIL 8   The Bible never disparages intellect and learning. Sometimes it warns us to avoid the wrong kind or to be sure that we do not allow reason to displace faith, but throughout the Scriptures there is a constant appeal to our sense of logic and our hunger for learning.

"Wisdom is the principle thing; therefore get wisdom; and with all thy getting get understanding" (Proverbs 4:7). The wisest man that ever lived said these words a thousand years before Christ. But nearly five hundred years before Solomon a man called Job who had lived under the most luxurious and the most appalling conditions expounded Solomon's proverb. He connected wisdom and understanding directly with our relationship to God and our moral standards: "Behold, the fear of the Lord, that is wisdom; and to depart from evil is understanding" (Job 28:28).

Wisdom apart from God, the source of supply, soon becomes bankrupt. Understanding that fails to distinguish between right and wrong rapidly deteriorates into confusion.

APRIL 9

Despite the non-conformists, the hermits, and and the beatnicks, it is true that most people appreciate the fact that they are part of a family. Perhaps that is one of the reasons the Christian faith is presented in terms of a family relationship: "Wherefore come out from among them, and be ye separate, saith the Lord, and touch not the unclean thing; and I will receive you, And will be a Father unto you, and ye shall be my sons and daughters, saith the Lord Almighty" (II Corinthians 6:17-18).

The Christian invitation is never simply negative, although in our preaching and living we often make it so. There is the necessity of a turning from sin that is involved in real faith, but far more important is the fact of turning to God.

When we do this, He not only separates us from our sins but He considers us to be members of His family. Our natural desire to be a member of a family is fully satisfied in the fellowship of the Divine Household.

APRIL 10

There are two kinds of fear. Animal fear is purely selfish. It is afraid of being hurt personally. Human fear may be little more than this and often is nothing more, but in addition to this selfish animal fear we are also capable of the kind that stems from our love for someone else. We can be dreadfully afraid lest we hurt the one we love.

When the Bible says that we should fear God often it is concerned with this latter unselfish emotion. We do not fear God simply because of His vengeance. We love Him so devotedly that we are afraid to do anything that would offend or bring reproach upon His Name.

This is what Peter preached to Cornelius: "In every nation he that feareth him, and worketh righteousness, is accepted with him" (Acts 10:35). These were people who loved God and feared lest they would do anything to offend Him. They feared God because they loved Him.

APRIL 11
It is difficult for us to realize that God is both a Father and a Judge. He is the Father of the righteous but the Judge of the unrighteous.

The Apostle Peter puts the two together in a single verse, "If ye call on the Father, who without respect of persons, judgeth according to every man's work, pass the time of your sojourning here in fear" (I Peter 1:17).

Although the judgment here refers to Christians and their works it is evident that the God who judges His own children will also judge the wicked with a severity and a finality that is almost impossible to comprehend. "That which beareth thorns and briars is rejected, and is nigh unto cursing; whose end is to be burned" (Hebrews 6:8).

What a privilege to come to God as a Father; how terrible to face Him as a Judge!

APRIL 12
God does not make men holy by magic. There is no simple formula that will produce an active saint.

The Bible makes it clear that once the Holy Spirit has done the work of regeneration and the "new creature" has been born, holiness depends a great deal upon the response of the individual to the commands of the Bible. Inevitably, this takes a long time and the process is still going on to the end of life and is completed only in eternity.

"Put off concerning the former conversation the old man and put on the new man, which after God is created in righteousness and true holiness" (Ephesians 4:22-24).

Victory can be instantaneous but the building of a holy character will take many years during which the child of God actively fashions his life in obedience to the Holy Spirit and relies implicitly on the power of God to enable him to do so.

APRIL 13 To be a real Christian it is necessary to be a non-conformist. The man whose life fits into the mould of this world is usually a stranger to the transforming power of God, or at best he is a poor specimen of Christianity.

The Bible says "Be not conformed to this world: but be ye transformed by the renewing of your mind" (Romans 12:2). There is a negative aspect to this change — non-conformity. There is also a positive aspect — transformation.

Non-conformity to the world is not Christianity. Many people who embrace other religions are non-conformists and some make a sort of religion out of their non-conformity.

The child of God does not conform to the world because he has been transformed. The new birth has given him a spiritual life that is not at home in the world and he finds his greatest happiness in the will of God rather than in the mould of the world.

APRIL 14 Deep within every human heart is an unquenchable thirst for life and a dreadful fear of dying. That is why we will go through hardship and privation rather than die. Anything to the human heart is better than death, but the most inevitable feature of life is death. The most uncertain thing that we possess is life.

The Bible says, "Wherefore, ye know not what shall lie on the morrow. For what is your life? It is even a vapour that appeareth for a little time, and then vanisheth away" (James 4:14).

The message of the Gospel urges men to turn to Jesus Christ and commit their limited human lives to Him and in return receive His unlimited Divine life: "And this is life eternal that they might know thee the only true God, and Jesus Christ, whom thou hast sent" (John 17:3).

Faith in Christ removes the finality of death and unrolls before us the horizon of eternity.

APRIL 15

Most religious skeptics have a Christian background. The greatest potential critic of the church is the man who has been reared in the midst of religious people or who is a religious leader himself.

Plutarch said: "Knavery is the best defense against a knave." And this is true of any area of life. The man who has been a part of a family, an army, an organization, or a church has by the fact of his close association been trusted with a knowledge of its strength and weakness.

If he has a degenerate nature and a perverted mind, he can come out of the group that has trusted him and criticize it as an outsider could never have done.

The Apostle Paul warned Timothy of this kind of person and urged him not to let it affect his faith in God: "This charge I commit unto thee . . . that thou by them mightest war a good warfare; Holding faith, and a good conscience; which some having put away concerning faith have made shipwreck" (I Timothy 1:18).

APRIL 16

The disciples of Jesus hoped to profit personally by their relationship to Him. They argued occasionally about who would have the best position in the kingdom.

Jesus made it clear to them that although there were spiritual blessings that would result from their loyalty to Him, Christianity in this world was essentially a life in which a man turned his back upon many things in his devotion to his Lord.

Jesus said, "If any man will come after me, let him deny himself, and take up his cross, and follow me" (Matthew 16:24).

In the modern church we have pictured Christianity as a sort of a bandwagon ride through life. Jesus pictured it as a life of self-denial in which the cross was always to be the central structure and Christ Himself the central figure.

APRIL 17 Everyone admits that murder is a sin, but few will recognize the fact that covetousness is also a sin. The Bible does not condemn one more than the other. The two sins are listed in the same passages of Scripture and carry with them the same penalty.

"The scripture hath concluded all under sin" (Galatians 3:22). This includes the man who murders and the man who covets; and "the soul that sinneth, it shall die" (Ezekiel 18:20).

This would be a hard Gospel if it did not also give the remedy for sin, "Wherefore lay apart all filthiness and superfluity of naughtiness, and receive with meekness the engrafted word, which is able to save your souls" (James 1:21).

APRIL 18 The people of God in this world are always in the minority. The entire Bible makes this clear.

There were only eight people who responded to the invitation of Noah and were saved from the flood. Abraham could not find even ten in the cities of Sodom and Gomorrah. Jesus taught that there are many headed for destruction and only a few turned toward life.

The gospel appeal goes out to everyone but only a few respond to it. "Many are called, but few are chosen" (Matthew 22:14).

The church of Sardis was typical of the world: "Thou hast a few names even in Sardis which have not defiled their garments" (Revelation 3:4).

When a man accepts the Gospel he chooses to walk a road that from the human standpoint may be lonely. In this world he will never belong to the majority. Real Christianity will never be popular.

The Christian will undoubtedly walk alone but he will not be lonely for he walks with God and his pathway leads to heaven.

APRIL 19 Most things in life are not inevitable. We have the privilege of making decisions about them. We can be business men or professional men, nurses or housewives. We can get married or remain single. These things are optional.

The Bible says that all of us have an inevitable appointment to keep with God — the judgment, "It is appointed unto men once to die, but after this the judgment" (Hebrews 9:27).

As surely as we must face death, we must all face the judgment. That is why it is so desperately important that we accept the salvation of God that has been provided in Christ. Then we are given credit for the righteousness that is in God's Son — the only righteousness that can stand before God.

APRIL 20 It is not only dangerous to hope for a second chance after death but is is contrary to the basic principles of the Bible.

The whole story of the rich man and Lazarus deals with the problem of a second chance, and the unmistakable conclusion is that there is none. "Between us and you there is a great gulf fixed; so that they which would pass from thence to you cannot; neither can they pass to us, that would come from thence" (Luke 16:26).

The story of the ten virgins strikes the same note of finality. The door was shut at midnight and the five foolish girls never got in.

Many times the Bible speaks of a day of harvest or an acceptable time to get right with God and warns of the peril involved in ignoring these opportunities. "For this shall every one that is godly pray unto thee in a time when thou mayest be found" (Psalm 32:6).

There is a day when the gulf is fixed, the door is shut, the harvest is ended, and the acceptable time is gone.

APRIL 21   The common denominator of all men is death. We are not born equal and we certainly do not live equally.

Some carry the asset of beauty through life while others fight the battle of ugliness. The rich may buy privileges that the poor cannot afford.

Lazarus longed for the crumbs which fell from the table while the rich man fared sumptuously. In life the wealthy man had many advantages, but his wealth, position, and power were impotent in the hour of death. The last enemy had finally equalized him and Lazarus.

The Bible declares, "We must needs die, and are as water spilt on the ground, which cannot be gathered up again: neither doth God respect any person" (II Samuel 14:14).

It is good for a man to be ready to live. It is absolutely essential that he be ready to die.

APRIL 22   The most dangerous thing about sin is that it usually appears in a rather glamorous, enticing form. It is presented to man with all of its immediate pleasures prominently displayed and its deadly fangs carefully concealed.

Sin comes to us dressed in its best clothes and it is often too late before we see the body of death that the clothes cover. On the outside there is excitement, adventure, popularity, wealth, satisfaction, and glamor, but the Bible warns us many times that the real essence of sin is boredom, monotony, loneliness, poverty, restlessness, and deformity.

"Stolen waters are sweet, and bread eaten in secret is pleasant. But he knoweth not that the dead are there; and that her guests are in the depths of hell" (Proverbs 9:17-18).

There is nothing attractive about naked sin. Jesus Christ came to save us from it and its penalty.

APRIL 23 Human life in the Bible is often compared in its durability to grass, and grass is usually the symbol of those things that are temporal. "All flesh is as grass, and all the glory of man as the flower of grass. The grass withereth, and the flower thereof falleth away" (I Peter 1:24).

The most beautiful bloom in the cultivated garden dies the same death as the common weed in the jungle. The prince and the beggar, the philosopher and the illiterate, the bushman and the civilized, live for a time and then inevitably go back to the dust from which they came.

Man is very conscious of his propensity toward decay and the cessation of life. That is why the message of the Gospel is so often focused around the miracle of new life in Christ — a life that can never fade. "He that hath the Son hath life; and he that hath not the Son of God hath not life" (I John 5:12).

APRIL 24 The Christian Bible presupposes the existence of a personal devil, and the man who accepts Christ as his Saviour is not a child of God for long before he comes into violent contact with Satan.

The world and the flesh would be harmless to the Christian if it were not for the temptations of the devil.

The Bible says, "Submit yourselves therefore to God: Resist the devil, and he will flee from you" (James 4:7).

Some people fail because they submit to God but do not resist. They do not burn their bridges behind them. Others fail because they resist but do not submit. They are attempting to fight a powerful foe without being under the command of the only power that has ever defeated the devil — the Lord Jesus Christ.

APRIL 25 When Jesus fed the five thousand He was dealing with a mob of people who were bored. Life had become monotonous and mundane. The wonder of living had been lost.

They had left their ordinary little lives and had followed Jesus into the wilderness, drawn by His miracles. In His presence their boredom was gone. The wonder returned and when they went back to their everyday tasks again there was a glow of glory about everything they did.

This is what the miracle of the new birth can do for any man or woman. Christianity does not change the world, but it changes people in the world. This is what the Apostle Paul was talking about when he said, "And whatsoever ye do in word or deed, do all in the name of the Lord Jesus, giving thanks to God and the Father by him" (Colossian 3:17).

APRIL 26 Parts of the Bible contain detailed instructions to be followed by a specific man at a particular time. God told Noah to build an ark and He gave Solomon an elaborate blueprint for a temple. Modern Christians are not to build arks or construct again the Jewish temple.

The Bible also lays down many fundamental principles that involve all men. These basic moral and spiritual laws never change. They are the same in the Old and New Testaments.

One of these latter precepts is that God never countenances sin and always judges it on some level. In the Old Testament Amos puts it this way: "Though they dig into hell, hence shall mine hand take them; though they climb up to heaven, thence will I bring them down" (Amos 9:2).

In the New Testament Paul expresses it more vehemently: "Unto them that are contentious, and do not obey the truth, but obey unrighteousness, indignation and wrath" (Romans 2:8).

APRIL 27 It is difficult to separate obedience from belief. Obedience to the teaching of the Bible and belief in the Gospel are almost synonymous in the Scriptures.

It is our faith in the Gospel that produces our salvation, but it is our obedience to the truth of the Gospel that is the evidence of our belief. If there is no obedience, the belief may be doubted. Our Lord urged His followers to respond to His call but always with a full awareness of the responsibilities that are involved.

Before a man accepts Christ he must realize that this presupposes that he rejects his sin. True, it is the Holy Spirit of God that will deliver him from his sin, but he comes to Christ in the first instance with this deliverance as one of his basic motives.

The Bible says, "He became the author of eternal salvation unto all them that obey him" (Hebrews 5:9).

APRIL 28 The false cults of the world could never launch their doctrines if they were not infiltrated with some elements of truth. That is why most of them at least start with the Bible. They lead their followers astray when they begin to add other books and traditions to the Bible, giving them equal authority.

The Word of God does not put its stamp of approval upon any other writing whether they be by preacher, prophet, or poet. Great minds have helped to clarify and interpret the Bible, but no man can add any revelation to the Bible.

It is the Word of God that is the cleansing agent in the life of the believer and it is the same Word that is the Truth for which man searches. Jesus prayed that His followers might be sanctified, but He promised no additional revelation of truth apart from the Word of God: "Sanctify them through thy truth: thy word is truth" (John 17:17).

APRIL 29 A Christian home is one in which the wall of discipline has been built. The Bible says, "Foolishness is bound in the heart of a child; but the rod of correction shall drive it far from him" (Proverbs 22:15).

The Bible also pictures the adult Christian as a soldier. The Apostle Paul uses this analogy, "Put on the whole armour of God" (Ephesians 6:11).

A soldier is governed by a code of discipline. He obeys the orders of a higher authority. The Christian soldier does not live according to his own dictates. His life is governed by the authority of the Bible. He obeys the commands of God.

The discipline of the Christian home should affect every member of the family, from the baby to the grandfather. Without it we do not have a Christian home.

APRIL 30 All men are born equal but all men are not the same. Some are born with a voice that is destined to fill opera halls. Others have vocal chords that will never produce music. Some are born to be tall. Others are destined to be short. Men are by no means equivalent to one another.

One of the supreme tests of my Christianity is my ability to love other Christians who are quite different from me. The Apostle of Love says, "We know that we have passed from death unto life, because we love the brethren" (I John 3:14).

Some people turn this verse around and try to make it say, "Because we love everyone we are Christians." But of course, this is not what it says. Our love for others does not *cause* our Christianity, it is the *effect* of our Christianity. We become the children of God by putting our faith in Christ. When we have done this, one of the results will be that we love all the other Christians.

MAY 1

It does not take much to separate one man from another. In this world we are all too familiar with the human apartheids — race, culture, morals, economics, education, and a host of others.

In addition to these, over which we have control and could overrule if we wished, there are the other dividing factors with which we have no means to cope — war, sickness, calamity, and death. One of the basic fears of man is to be separated from those he loves. One of the tragic deformities of man is his propensity to separate himself from other men.

No wonder the early Christians rejoiced in the fact that their simple faith in Jesus Christ gave them an interest in the love of God from which they could never more be separated. "For I am persuaded, that neither death nor life, nor angels nor principalities, nor powers nor things present, nor things to come, nor height, nor depth, nor any other creature, shall be able to separate us from the love of God, which is in Christ Jesus our Lord" (Romans 8:38-39).

MAY 2

The story of the rich farmer describes a man who made a great many excellent plans but left God out completely.

He had been blessed so much that he decided to begin an elaborate building program on his farm, but God called him a fool because he failed to include Him in his plans.

In the Old Testament a man was similarly blessed. He, too, had reaped a great harvest, and he had stopped to consider what he should do with it. In his case, self was entirely forgotten and God was glorified, for he says, "What shall I render unto the Lord for all his benefits toward me?" (Psalm 116:12).

The foolish man plans for himself and neglects God. The wise man keeps God in the center of his plans and gives the glory to God.

MAY 3

The Bible proclaims that the Rock of the Christian Church is Jesus Christ.

The Psalmist prophesied it, "The stone which the builders refused is become the head stone of the corner" (Psalm 118:22).

Isaiah reaffirmed it, "Behold I lay in Zion for a foundation stone, a tried stone, a precious corner stone, a sure foundation" (Isaiah 28:16).

Peter preached it, "This is the stone which was set at nought of you builders, which is become the head of the corner" (Acts 4:11).

Paul proclaimed it, "And are built upon the foundation of the apostles and prophets, Jesus Christ himself being the chief corner stone" (Ephesians 2:20).

The person who does not rest his cause completely on Jesus Christ is not a part of the Church because the Church is built on Christ. "All other ground is sinking sand."

MAY 4

This world without Christ has gradually worked its way into a deplorable condition. We have sin that we cannot cure and science that we cannot control. We fight to end all wars and we only succeed in setting the stage for greater wars. The material world has a magnificent potential but man with his corruption has turned it into an abode of fear.

Man is broken and he needs mending. He is fickle and he needs stabilizing. He is weak and he needs strengthening. He is sinking and he needs to be lifted.

Only God can set man right. The Apostle Peter knew this and as he pronounced his benediction he gave voice to it, "The God of all grace, who hath called us unto his eternal glory by Christ Jesus, after that ye have suffered a while, make you perfect, stablish, strengthen, settle you" (I Peter 5:10).

MAY 5

For the ordinary person the period immediately preceding the Second Coming of Christ will be no different from the life to which he has been accustomed. World conditions will have changed and the prophetic signs will have appeared but the Bible indicates that the average person will be living out his life as usual.

"As it was in the days of Lot; they did eat, they drank, they bought, they sold; they planted, they builded" (Luke 17:28). Twenty-four hours before the brimstone rained from heaven a banner could have been strung across Sodom and Gomorrah announcing, "Business As Usual."

Jesus declared, "Even thus shall it be in the day when the Son of man is revealed" (Luke 17:30).

We need to make sure we are right with God when life is still going along normally. If we wait until judgment begins to fall, we will have waited too long.

MAY 6

It is difficult for most people to realize that the work of salvation has already been done. Nothing can be added to it. The sacrifice of Christ on the cross was complete. Man's efforts can add nothing to it nor take anything from it. When Jesus cried out, "It is finished" (John 19:30), He meant just what He said. The efforts of man cannot do more than the death of Christ has already done.

Jesus said, "My meat is to do the will of him that sent me, and to finish his work" (John 4:34).

That is why the Apostle Paul said, "A man is not justified by the works of the law, but by the faith of Jesus Christ" (Galatians 2:16).

The verb of heathen religions is *do* and their devotees spend their days trying. The verb of the Christian religion is *done* and God's people spend their lives trusting.

MAY 7 Every person is the subject of a master — the follower of a leader. He belongs to God or he belongs to Satan.

Either he has taken his stand for Jesus Christ or he has taken his stand against Him and on the side of Satan. He is the child of God or the child of the devil. "No man can serve two masters: for either he will hate the one, and love the other; or else he will hold to the one, and despise the other. Ye cannot serve God and mammon" (Matthew 6:24).

The wise man will make sure that he has renounced the devil and turned to God.

MAY 8 In his gospel, the Apostle John said that God loved the world so much that He gave His Son to save it. This would indicate that there is nothing basically sinful about the world.

In his epistle, the same man said, "Love not the world, neither the things that are in the world. If any man love the world, the love of the Father is not in him" (I John 2:15). This verse would lead us to condemn the world as evil.

The Apostle Paul explains the evil characteristic of a world that is not basically evil when he says that man "worshipped and served the creature more than the Creator" (Romans 1:25).

The world becomes a foe when man loves it to the extent that he cannot see the hand of God back of it, and his love of the world has eclipsed his love of God. The man who does not lay the measurements of eternity over every half hour of his life is a worldly man. He is worshiping and living for the material and temporal rather than the spiritual and eternal.

MAY 9

Death seldom blows a trumpet to announce his approach. It is true that the aged and the infirm may be more conscious of his imminence, but no one is immune. It is not uncommon for the senior members of the family to outlive the junior or for those who are seriously diseased to bury those who have been remarkably healthy.

The Bible says, "For man also knoweth not his time: as the fishes that are taken in an evil net, and as the birds that are caught in the snare; so are the sons of men snared in an evil time, when it falleth suddenly upon them" (Ecclesiastes 9:12).

No man has a premium on life in this world, but God offers to every man an insurance policy on everlasting life in the next. The only condition that is set is that he turn from his sin and trust the Saviour.

MAY 10

Hezekiah was a good man, but toward the end of his life God sent a prophet to him with this warning, "Set thine house in order; for thou shalt die, and not live" (II Kings 20:1).

Many good people need the same advice. Sometimes it is the financial house that needs adjusting. With others it is the marital house that has slipped. It might be the moral house or the social house or the educational house. Most men would like to be sure that all these areas of life are in order before they meet God.

The person who is separated from God needs to set his spiritual house in order. He needs to repent of his sin and turn to God's Son for deliverance and salvation. Otherwise he is not prepared to meet God and should he die he will face the dire consequences of a life lived in a house that was never set in order.

MAY 11   There are many indications of the end of the age, but the exact time is not known. The Bible compares it to a woman who expects a child. She determines an approximate date, but as it approaches she prepares herself for the event at a moment's notice. "Then sudden destruction cometh upon them, as travail upon a woman with child" (I Thessalonians 5:13).

We know that this age will be terminated and that Christ will return. We also know some of the signs of His coming, but we are totally ignorant of the exact hour. The advice of the Bible is to be prepared for His coming at any time. "Watch ye therefore: for ye know not when the master of the house cometh, at even, or at midnight, or at the cock-crowing, or in the morning" (Mark 13:35).

Few people look at the complex problems of the modern world without realizing that it must end sometime, but thousands of people are completely unprepared for the end.

MAY 12   If a man is going the wrong way, three areas of his life must be affected before the error is rectified. Intellectually — he must realize his mistake. Emotionally — he must be disturbed by his stupidity. Volitionally — he must reverse his direction.

The Bible says, "God commandeth all men everywhere to repent" (Acts 17:30).

To do this our intellects must be convicted. We will never turn to God unless we realize that we are wrong. Then there will be a conviction that touches our emotion. We will be upset and sorry for our sin.

Both of these could happen and we might still fall short of regeneration. The convicting power of the Holy Spirit must saturate our powers of volition to such a degree that we determine with the Prodigal, "I will arise and go" (Luke 15:18).

MAY 13 God does not arbitrarily condemn anyone nor save anyone. For some reason, man has been left as a free moral agent to make for himself the most important decision of his life.

Salvation has been made available to man and the Bible is filled with urgency in its invitations to all men to accept the provision made and enter eternity prepared to meet God.

Jesus said to the Jewish people, "Ye will not come to me, that ye might have life" (John 5:40). In the Old Testament God said, "I have called, and ye refused; I have stretched out my hand, and no man regarded" (Proverbs 1:24).

This is now the invitation that is extended to all, but it is man's responsibility to accept it and turn to God.

MAY 14 It is difficult to describe sin because it is many times worse than anything to which we might compare it.

We might say that sin is like the devil, and this brings before our minds many loathsome pictures, but sin is more intense in its evil power than the devil. It was this awful force (which we describe in the English language with a harmless looking little three-letter word) that caused the fall of the devil.

We might add that sin is like hell, but again we have only partially uncovered an ugly sore. It was sin that made hell necessary and without this damning poison there would be no hell.

Death with all its miseries and uncertainties and agonies is not as vicious as sin because it owes its dreadful existence to sin.

This is the condemnation of all men — sin. The Bible says, "If we say that we have no sin, we deceive ourselves, and the truth is not in us" (I John 1:8).

MAY 15 Faith is like a door that leads to God. On the material side of the door are the words, "The just shall live by faith" (Romans 1:17).

When a man takes a step of faith and gives himself to God, it is as if he walked through the door, but when he looks back on the other side of the door, he sees the words, "I know whom I have believed, and am persuaded that he is able to keep that which I have committed unto him against that day" (II Timothy 1:12).

Faith is the way to God. Knowledge comes as a result of an experience with God.

MAY 16 The entire Bible has a message for everyone, but there are some passages that are not addressed to everyone.

Sometimes the command is to an individual, sometimes to a special nation, and often to some particular kind of person.

However, much of the Bible is universal in its appeal. When Paul wrote to Titus many of the things he said applied to everyone, "The grace of God that bringeth salvation hath appeared to all men" (Titus 2:11).

This is a message for the whole world. That does not mean that all men will eventually be saved, but that God has made provision for the salvation of all men.

In Canada the government provides a pension for all senior citizens. When they reach a certain age the pension is there waiting for them. However, they must send in an application before they actually get it.

Salvation is for all of us. No one is excluded, but it does not actually become ours until we apply to God through simple faith in Christ.

MAY 17

In the Bible the end of the world is described in terms of a wedding feast. Ten young women were invited. Five of them got in and the other five were shut out because they came too late.

Jesus said the first five were wise. They were prepared for the feast. The other five were foolish. They were not ready.

"Afterward came also the other virgins, saying, Lord, Lord, open to us. But He answered and said, Verily I say unto you, I know you not" (Matthew 25:11-12).

You and I are numbered by God among the wise if we have committed our lives to Christ — the foolish if we have never done so.

MAY 18

Man builds his life for eternity. Every day he adds to his building. Some build large, some small. Some build well, some poorly, but everyone builds.

In the gospel of Matthew Jesus said that the most important part of the building is its foundation. If the foundation is right, the building stands; if it is wrong, the building falls.

The life that is built on the rock endures the day of judgment. The life that is built on the sand is condemned. It may be a moral building, an intellectual building, or a religious building, but it stands or falls on the merits of its foundation.

The Bible says, "Other foundation can no man lay than that is laid, which is Jesus Christ" (I Corinthians 3:11).

Religion is good, the church is valuable, and morality is commendable, but the only foundation that will stand the test of judgment is Jesus Christ. If a man has trusted Christ, he is on the Rock. If he has not trusted Christ, he is on the sand.

MAY 19

There is nothing in the Bible to indicate that a person is held responsible for every evil scene that passes before his eyes or for every thought that is suggested to his mind, but the Word of God does warn against the sin of harboring sinful ideas.

It is one thing to think casually about something; it is an entirely different thing to allow the idea to lodge in the mind and to meditate on it.

The Psalmist said, "If I regard iniquity in my heart, the Lord will not hear me" (Psalm 66:18).

Thoughts that are nourished inevitably result in action. That is why the Apostle Paul said, "Whatsoever things are true, whatsoever things are honest, whatsoever things are just, whatsoever things are pure, whatsoever things are lovely, whatsoever things are of good report . . . think on these things" (Philippians 4:8).

MAY 20

It is possible for a man to be a great philanthropist throughout his life but to go to meet his Maker without any merit of any kind. The Apostle Paul said, "Though I bestow all my goods to feed the poor . . . and have not charity, it profiteth me nothing" (I Corinthians 13:3).

This verse ruins forever the hope of the man who is depending upon his good deeds to outweigh his bad deeds and bring him salvation.

The word "charity" means "love" and the message of this entire chapter is that all the human virtues are of no value apart from love. This is not mere fleshly passion or human compassion. This is that Divine Love that comes into a man's life when he is born into the family of God. The Bible says, "Love is of God; and every one that loveth is born of God, and knoweth God" (I John 4:7).

The humanitarian may give until it hurts, but it "profiteth him nothing" until he has accepted God's Son as his Saviour.

MAY 21 The Bible says, "Work out your own salvation with fear and trembling" (Philippians 2:12).

If nothing followed these words, we might conclude that we could proceed to formulate our own plan of salvation and live our lives perfecting it. Some people do this, and of course they fail.

The next verse explains it, "For it is God which worketh in you both to will and to do of his good pleasure" (Philippians 2:13). Nothing can be worked out until it is first worked in. Salvation is of the Lord. God gives it to us freely through His Son. We do nothing to merit it. We simply receive it.

Once we have salvation, we can begin to work it out through our every day lives. Until we accept salvation as the free gift of God we have nothing on the inside to work out.

MAY 22 Take care of time, and eternity will take care of itself. Why anticipate heaven and why worry about hell? This is the advice of the world and the flesh and the devil.

The Bible reverses the formula and puts the emphasis not upon time but eternity. It urges man to escape the wrath of God and to be prepared for heaven.

Life is described in the Bible as short, uncertain, and unimportant in the light of eternity. "My days are like a shadow that declineth; and I am withered like grass" (Psalm 102:11).

It is possible to be prepared for this world but not for the next. It is impossible to be prepared for the next world and not for this. You can be ready to live without being ready to die. You cannot be ready to die without being ready to live. An aircraft that can carry me a hundred miles may not be able to carry me a thousand, but if I am sure it can carry me a thousand then I know it can easily handle the hundred.

In terms of eternity how effective is your aircraft?

MAY 23   There are no spiritual giants in the sight of God — only spiritual babies.

The disparity between the holiness of God and the holiness of the most outstanding saint is so great that they cannot be compared. If it were not for the grace of God, no one would be saved, but because of His matchless grace God receives us when we come to Him through Christ.

The inspired writers were all aware of the fact that even the best man would deserve judgment apart from God's mercy. If this is true, what about the worst man?

"If the righteous scarcely be saved, where shall the ungodly and the sinner appear?" (I Peter 4:18). This does not mean that such a one cannot be saved, but it does infer the severity of his judgment if he is not saved.

MAY 24   Suffering temporarily for the sake of lasting relief is accepted as a sensible procedure. This is the basis of all medical operations or the consumption of medicines that have a bitterly undesirable taste. We are willing to undergo immediate pain because it brings permanent peace.

To some extent this is true spiritually. The Christian life is hard. It involves considerable tribulation and suffering, but beyond these present difficulties is the hope of eternal blessedness.

When a man accepts Jesus Christ he faces the challenge of the cross, but he also becomes the possessor of a steadfast hope that carries him through: "For I reckon that the sufferings of this present time are not worthy to be compared with the glory which shall be revealed in us" (Romans 8:18).

Boiled down to simple terms the Gospel says: Reject Christ now and face the condemnation of God forever. Accept the tribulations of a Christian life now and look forward to the blessing of God forever.

MAY 25 The Bible reveals God as "the God of all grace" and "the God of all comfort" (I Peter 5:10 and II Corinthians 1:3).

We do not work with people for long before we become impatient with them and indifferent to their needs. The resources of heaven are inexhaustible. God works and never wearies; He gives and is never poorer. There is an infinite variety in the Divine storehouse — something for every man's need and sufficient for the needs of every man.

After Jesus had fed over five thousand people, the Bible says, "And they took up of the fragments that remained twelve baskets full" (Matthew 14:20).

No one went away hungry that day. No one ever comes to Jesus Christ and goes away dissatisfied. He is the God of all grace and all comfort.

MAY 26 The Prophet Habakkuk probably lived six hundred years before Jesus was born, but it is quite clear that he was more interested in salvation through faith in Christ than many who have lived during this age of grace in which this Gospel is being preached.

Some of the eagerness of the Prophet can be sensed in his words, "I will stand upon my watch, and set me upon my tower, and will watch to see what he will say unto me" (Habakkuk 2:1). And his longing for the truth was rewarded by a revelation of the Gospel of Faith: "The just shall live by his faith" (Habakkuk 2:4).

In his day the world was rather dimly lit by revelation, but he was determined to find his way to the truth and God revealed it to him. Our world is ablaze with the revelation of God in Christ, but thousands have deliberately turned their backs to the light and prefer to live in the darkness.

The message of the Gospel is: Turn, look, live!

MAY 27 Religion that does not make us glad does us little good. The Bible is a book of joy.

Nehemiah urged his people to stop crying with the words, "The joy of the Lord is your strength" (Nehemiah 8:10). Ezra pointed out the joy that filled the hearts of the people when they finished rebuilding the temple. "The Lord hath made them joyful" (Ezra 6:22).

Jesus told His disciples that a part of His mission was to bring them His joy. "These things have I spoken unto you, that my joy might remain in you, and that your joy might be full" (John 15:11).

Joy does not necessitate the absence of sorrow or pain or trial. It does involve a divine happiness through Jesus Christ even in the midst of these things.

If our religion has no power to bless us with gladness, there is something wrong either with the completeness of our surrender to Christ or in the articles of our faith.

MAY 28 Animals are content if their physical appetites are satisfied. We have no reason to believe that they expect or need anything else.

The history of the human race proves many times over that material sustenance is necessary to man but it by no means satisfies him. There is a constant longing in the heart of man that reaches out beyond the world of things and craves for the spiritual food that will feed and satisfy his soul. That is why all men are religious.

God explained this to His people in the wilderness and Jesus repeated it in response to the temptation of Satan, "Man doth not live by bread only, but by every word that proceedeth out of the mouth of the Lord doth man live" (Deuteronomy 8:3, Matthew 4:4, Luke 4:4).

Without God man is dead spiritually and his soul is starved. With God he lives spiritually and his soul is satisfied.

MAY 29 The Christian is founded on Christ as a building rests upon a rock: "The foundation of God standeth sure, having this seal, The Lord knoweth them that are his" (II Timothy 2:19).

He is rooted in Christ, as a tree is rooted in the earth from which it draws its nourishment: "As ye have therefore received Christ Jesus the Lord, so walk ye in him: Rooted and built up in him" (Colossians 2:6, 7).

He is united with Christ as a branch in the vine from which it draws its life: "As the branch cannot bear fruit of itself, except it abide in the vine; no more can ye, except ye abide in me" (John 15:4).

Before a man trusts Christ as his Saviour he is restless in a changing world, hungry in a barren civilization, and dead in a sinful life. Jesus Christ gives him permanent stability, abundant nourishment and eternal life.

MAY 30 Popularity is a fairly accurate gauge of our relationship with God. It is impossible for a Christian to live for God and have no opposition from the world.

Sometimes opposition comes at home, sometimes in business, sometimes in society, but come it will. If there is no objection to anything we do, it is because we are not really Christians or we are not living as Christians should live.

The man who walks with God goes against the world. The man who talks with God has a different vocabulary than the world. The man who loves God is hated by the world.

Jesus said, "Woe unto you, when all men shall speak well of you! for so did their fathers to the false prophets" (Luke 6:26).

How does the thermometer of popularity register in our lives?

MAY 31 Sin is a spiritual sickness that demands the medicinal power of the shed blood.

Isaiah described the sin of his people in vivid terms of disease, "The whole head is sick and the whole heart faint. From the sole of the foot even unto the head there is no soundness in it; but wounds, and bruises, and putrifying sores" (Isaiah 1:6).

In this picture, sinful man becomes a helpless, hopeless individual indeed, and it is in this very context that the Bible presents the sufferings and death of the Saviour as the antidote for the sickness of sin: "The Spirit of the Lord is upon me; because he hath anointed me to preach the gospel to the poor; he hath sent me to heal the broken-hearted, to preach deliverance to the blind, to set at liberty them that are bruised" (Luke 4:18).

No amount of trying or giving or working will cure the malady of the human heart. Only a personal committal of a diseased soul to the Saviour will result in a cure that will last forever.

JUNE 1   The Christian life involves compensations and tribulations. Before accepting Christ we should be attracted by the blessings but we should be alerted to the afflictions.

God never promises the Christian deliverance from tribulation, but He does guarantee Divine power in the midst of trouble. Paul chided the Thessalonians because they had become restless under their trials, "No man should be moved by these afflictions: for yourselves know that we are appointed thereunto" (I Thessalonians 3:3).

In this world our walk with God includes a constant warfare against the world. The struggle does not end and the arms are never laid down until God calls us from this field of battle into His presence.

Accept Christ and at the same time accept the challenge of the greatest conflict you have ever known.

JUNE 2   Christian grace is not demonstrated by being nice to nice people, lovely to lovable people, or sweet to sweet people. The Christian should undergo such a complete transformation of life and character that he can be nice to nasty people, lovely to hateful people, and sweet to sour people. "For this is thankworthy, if a man for conscience toward God endure grief, suffering wrongfully" (I Peter 2:19).

Man in the natural finds this impossible. He may put forth a valiant effort, struggle heroically, but he will fail miserably. His humanity eventually forces its way to the top and he fights back.

Only after a personal experience with Jesus Christ that has worked in our lives the miracle of regeneration can we hope to live as God expects a Christian to live.

We do not lose the old instinct but God gives us a new, divine, spiritual life that is more powerful than the old human life.

JUNE 3 Midnight is the point of time that marks the end of one day and the beginning of another. It is a word that signifies the closing of a given period and the opening of a new era.

It will be midnight when our opportunity of accepting Jesus Christ as our Saviour is gone, and we are ushered into eternity with God or without God — the midnight that terminates the day of grace and begins the eternity of justice.

The five foolish virgins came after midnight only to find that the door had been shut and when Jesus told the story He concluded with these words, "Watch therefore, for ye know neither the day nor the hour wherein the Son of man cometh" (Matthew 25:13).

JUNE 4 The first five books of the New Testament are historical accounts of the life of Jesus and the apostles. The last twenty-two books contain the teaching ministry.

Out of these only 15 chapters are addressed to individuals. The other 128 chapters are addressed to churches and groups of Christians. If you had lived during the first century and had refused to go to church you would have missed almost 90 per cent of the teaching found in the New Testament even if you had been the sole recipient of the personal letters.

It is no wonder, then, that the author of Hebrews says to consider one another, "not forsaking the assembling of yourselves together, as the manner of some is" (Hebrews 10:25).

The church is a spiritual building that is manifest to the world in a physical assembly. The only way to become a member of the church is to be born into it through faith in Christ and the essential way to receive the majority of the teaching of the Bible for the church is to assemble with its physical members on earth.

JUNE 5

The day of judgment becomes a solemn occasion when we realize the nature of the Judge.

It would not be difficult to be judged by a pastor or Sunday school teacher or relative. These are all as human as you and I and subject to the power of sin. However, the Bible says that the One before whom we will stand and give an account is infinitely holy, "God is light, and in him is no darkness at all" (I John 1:5).

God has never sinned and has never excused sin. Unless we have trusted in the finished work of Jesus Christ on Calvary's cross, we will stand before God without excuse. If we have trusted Christ we will stand forgiven, "He that believeth on him is not condemned" (John 3:18).

JUNE 6

Sometimes sin is passed off as a form of insanity. It is quite true that an insane person may do some sinful things but insanity and sin are far from synonymous terms.

Insanity is a physical thing produced by the structure of a man's body and nerves and brain. Sin is a spiritual force that can produce insane results from a human mechanism that is perfect.

Insanity is a disease for which man cannot be held responsible. Sin is a human tragedy of enormous proportions for which God does make man accountable. The person who is mentally ill cannot turn his back on his misfortune any more than he could decide to walk away from his cancer or heart disease, but the sinner can turn in faith to Christ and leave his sin behind.

The Bible says, "Let the wicked forsake his way, and the unrighteous man his thoughts: and let him return unto the Lord, and he will have mercy upon him, and to our God, for he will abundantly pardon" (Isaiah 55:7).

JUNE 7

No sensible person can guarantee that he will be alive tomorrow morning. All men, of all classes, creeds and colors, are united in the certainty of death.

The Bible says, "For he seeth that wise men die, likewise the fool and the brutish person perish, and leave their wealth to others" (Psalm 49:10).

Through faith in Jesus Christ we can someday share in His resurrection and have personal victory over death. The Bible warns of the inevitability of death many times, but it also assures us of the possibility of life.

The Apostle Paul says that the grace of God "Is now made manifest by the appearing of our Saviour Jesus Christ, who hath abolished death, and hath brought life and immortality to light through the gospel" (II Timothy 1:10).

JUNE 8

The mercy of God is without limit and His grace is inexhaustible, but our ability to avail ourselves of these is dependent upon the conditions that God has laid down.

The grace of God is big enough for anyone, but there is no room in it for the man who refuses to turn from his sin. The mercy of God is "from everlasting to everlasting" but only the repentant sinner can avail himself of it.

In the Old Testament God continually urged the people to come and accept His favor, but it is quite clear that unless they were willing to leave their sin behind them they could not come. Moreover, God would not even hear their cry: "Then shall they cry unto the Lord, but he will not hear them: he will even hide his face from them at that time, as they have behaved themselves ill in their doings" (Micah 3:4).

The only thing that can prevent the cry of man from reaching the ear of God is sin. When we are ready to turn from our sin the wave length to heaven is wide open.

JUNE 9

The Old and New Testaments are inseparable. What the Prophets prophesied, the Apostles preached. The themes of the Prophets are identical to the messages of the Apostles. The only difference is the tense of the verbs. One spoke in the future tense, the other in the past.

Peter clarifies this fact, "Unto us they (prophets) did minister the things, which are now reported unto you by them (apostles) that have preached the gospel unto you" (I Peter 1:12).

Prophecy is condensed, outlined Gospel. Gospel is expanded, applied Prophecy. The Christ of the Apostles fills the pages of the Old Testament. The Messiah of the Prophets walks through the pages of the New Testament. The man who sees any part of the Bible should see Christ, and the man who knows Christ personally knows God.

JUNE 10

Hope involves desire and expectation. The Christian hope includes man's deepest longings and an assurance that they will be realized. The Apostle Peter called it a "lively hope." He described it as "an inheritance, incorruptible and undefiled, and that fadeth not away" (I Peter 1:34).

In this life almost the opposite is true. Joy and beauty and value are marred by sorrow, ugliness, and vanity. Wheat shares its nourishment with tares, thorns appear on the same branch with roses, sunlight is silhouetted by shadows, health fights a losing battle with disease, and laughter creates the wrinkle that guides our tears.

Included in the Christian's inheritance is a place where love knows no hatred, hope contains no fear, purity has no cause for doubt, songs are never followed by sighs, and light needs no darkness. Without Christ there is no hope. With Christ hope is a dream come true.

JUNE 11

Pity is care for the weak. Compassion is care for the suffering. Mercy is care for the undeserving.

All of these are part of God's plan for salvation. Sinful man is weak and needs God's strength. He suffers from the ravages of his sin and needs his wounds mollified. He has spent his life going away from God and therefore needs mercy.

After his appalling experience with a wife who became a prostitute, Hosea went to the public market and bought her back and forgave her. This Old Testament Prophet and the New Testament Apostles compare this to the love of God for sinful man, "I will have mercy upon her that had not obtained mercy. Not by works of righteousness which we have done, but according to his mercy he saved us" (Hosea 2:23; Titus 3:5).

We have sinned. God is merciful. Our salvation is determined by our response to the mercy of God.

JUNE 12

The world has always been familiar with the tragedy of displaced people — the Jews in Babylon, the Greeks in Rome, and the wandering multitudes in Europe after the havoc of World War II.

Man craves for the privilege of belonging. That is why he joins clubs and lodges and churches. He wants to be a part of something. But in a sense the worldly man never belongs because everything he joins eventually passes away. The organizations and the nations of this world are transitory.

When we accept Jesus Christ as our Saviour we are born into the family of God and become citizens of the Kingdom of God. Then, for the first time, we become a part of something that will last forever. We are no longer "displaced people"; we are God's people: "Which in time past were not a people, but are now the people of God" (I Peter 2:10).

Without the Lord man is displaced. With Him man belongs.

JUNE 13   Although science cannot prove the existence of God, man is not left without any signposts that point in the direction of a Supreme Being.

The Bible says, "The heavens declare the glory of God" (Psalm 19:1). They do not prove God but they point to God.

The material world does the same thing, "For the invisible things of him from the creation of the world are clearly seen, being understood by the things that are made, even his eternal power and Godhead" (Romans 1:20). Everyone is surrounded by things that point in the direction of a creator. They do not prove God, but they do point to God.

The man who ignores these signposts of life and hangs his future on the uncertain hook of atheism is foolish indeed. The Bible says, "The fool hath said in his heart, There is no God" (Psalm 14:1).

JUNE 14   Man can paint the future only with the colors supplied by the present. That is why most of our descriptions of heaven and the future life are in the form of negatives — no death, no tears, no pain, no darkness.

We paint pictures of the future on the miserable little canvasses of the present and they are always inadequate. Beauties are never diminished, tasks are never monotonous, tastes are never insipid, and fellowship is never ended.

With the language of earth it is impossible to describe the glories of heaven. The vocabulary of the material world is too limited to express the realities of the spiritual universe.

The Bible says, "Eye hath not seen, nor ear heard, neither have entered into the heart of man, the things which God hath prepared for them that love him" (I Corinthians 2:9).

We fail in our attempts to describe these things but the Word of God is clear in revealing the way to have them. The basic essential is a love for God that accepts His Son as Saviour.

JUNE 15   The Bible compares the religious experience of the Christian to death, burial, and resurrection.

When a man trusts Christ as his Saviour and commits his life to God, he considers himself dead to his former life of sin and worldliness. If he is wise, he will bury the old life, by removing himself as far away from its influence as is practicably possible.

Finally, he will begin to cultivate the new life, the spiritual life that God has given him.

The Bible says, "Knowing this, that our old man is crucified with him, that the body of sin might be destroyed, that henceforth we should not serve sin . . . even so we also should walk in newness of life" (Romans 6:6, 4).

JUNE 16   The term "Christian" is used only three times in the New Testament. Today we use it frequently and loosely. We talk of Christian nations, Christian institutions, and Christian people. As a matter of fact, anyone who believes in God and has committed no major crime is considered a Christian.

The Bible draws the lines much more closely. Certainly, a Christian must be a member of God's family and the Bible makes it clear that there are many people who are not in this category. "For as many as are led by the Spirit of God, they are the sons of God" (Romans 8:14).

I became a son when I was born into my father's family, and the only way I could become a son of God was to be born into God's family.

Many nice people who look like Christians and who do some of the things Christians do have never been born again into the spiritual family of God. The world may call these people Christians, but the Bible says that they become the children of God only by virtue of the new birth.

JUNE 17 The cross minus the empty tomb would be little more than a dead religious emblem.

In His own words, Jesus calls Himself the Good Shepherd with particular reference to His death on the cross. In the Epistle to the Hebrews He is called the Great Shepherd with special emphasis laid upon His resurrection, "Now the God of peace, that brought again from the dead our Lord Jesus Christ that great shepherd of the sheep" (Hebrews 13:20).

The cross assures us of the forgiveness of God. The empty tomb assures us of the future with God. Because Christ died we have happiness now in the confidence of knowing we are right with God. Because Christ rose we have hope for eternity because we share in the life of our Lord. When we become His, Christ's eternal life becomes ours.

JUNE 18 Every religion respects its priests. The Roman Catholics think of a priest with extreme awe and affection. Protestants think of their ministers as men ordained by God. Jews look to their rabbis as religious authorities.

In the Jewish faith, however, there is a sense in which every man is the priest for his own household — in the offering of the Paschal Lamb. God told Moses, "Ye shall be unto me a kingdom of priests" (Exodus 19:6).

Peter applied this title to all those who had trusted Jesus Christ as Saviour; he called them "a royal priesthood" (I Peter 2:9). The message in these words is that any man can go directly to God through God's Son. No other human mediator is necessary. "In Jesus Christ our Lord we have boldness and access with confidence" (Ephesians 3:11, 12).

The Christian needs no human priest. For confession, for forgiveness, for restoration, and for salvation there is only one Priest, the Lord Jesus Christ. Go to Him and you reach God.

JUNE 19 There are three kinds of prodigals mentioned in the Bible.

The Apostate may never have been saved and is typified by Judas. There is the man of God who has made a serious blunder — like David in the Old Testament and Peter in the New. There is the lukewarm Christian who has made no serious mistake but has gradually deteriorated spiritually. The Apostle Thomas would be a good example of this.

The important thing for the backslider to know is that God the Father wants him to come back and has provided a way for him to do it. The Bible says, "If we confess our sins, he is faithful and just to forgive us our sins, and to cleanse us from all unrighteousness" (I John 1:9).

JUNE 20 The words of a popular song say: "I'm sitting on top of the world." It is one thing to sing about it; it is quite another thing to do it.

Many people let the world sit on top of them. They are like the pictures of the strong man with the world resting on his shoulders.

In one sense life may be described as a battle between man and the world. The politics and economics, wars and diseases, business and society of the world press in upon us from all sides.

Man is incapable of handling all of these things adequately. He tries desperately. He succeeds occasionally but eventually the world gets him down.

The people in the days of Jesus faced this same human struggle for survival and Jesus promised them victory. "In the world ye shall have tribulation: but be of good cheer; I have overcome the world" (John 16:33). This is true for us as it was for them. The Apostle Paul assures us that the victory of Christ over the world can be ours when we put our faith in Him.

JUNE 21 The fifth chapter of Romans is introduced by declaring that we can be justified by faith and as a result have "peace with God."

Faith in Christ brings about the immediate removal of sin and with sin out of the way the hostility between man and God is gone. Peace has been made.

When we have made our peace with God, a divine miracle imparts to us the peace of God. This is what gives the Christian stability in a tottering world, calmness in a raging sea, and hope in a desperate situation.

The Bible promises, "Great peace have they which love thy law; and nothing shall offend them" (Psalm 119:165).

The peace of God will be essential to your moral sanity in the days that are ahead, but you can never realize it until you have made your peace with God through faith in Jesus Christ.

JUNE 22 Napoleon carved his name in the history books of the world with military genius. Khrushchev wormed his way to the top through political intrigue and his name appears on the front pages of the world newspapers. Churchill out-thought, out-worked, and out-ran his contemporaries, and his name will out-live others in the annals of the Second World War. Eisenhower endeared himself in the hearts of the American people and his name will always appear among the Presidents of the United States.

The Christian was chosen by God before the foundation of the world and his name is written in the Lamb's Book of Life. The Old Testament declares, "The Lord thy God hath chosen thee to be a special people unto himself, above all people that are upon the face of the earth" (Deuteronomy 7:6).

Both Paul and Peter confirm this covenant with the Christian Church, "He hath chosen us in him before the foundation of the world" (Ephesians 1:4).

It is a fine thing to be selected by man. It is a much better thing to be chosen by God.

JUNE 23 It is difficult for the heart of man to forgive but, changed by the power of God, it is possible. It is virtually impossible for the mind of man to forget.

We may forgive someone for an immoral blunder, but although we reinstate him into our society, we rarely see him but that we also see his mistake. Our jails and penitentiaries release a criminal after he has served his time, and we say he is a free man, but his criminal record follows him to his grave.

The heart of David must have leaped within him when God revealed to him the Divine attitude toward sin, "As far as the east is from the west, so far hath he removed our transgressions from us" (Psalm 103:12).

Man forgives but never forgets; God forgives and forever forgets.

JUNE 24 Empires and nations develop characteristics by which they will always be remembered. Greece was cultural, Babylon was commercial, Rome was military, the United States is pragmatic, and Israel was religious.

The Jew who is not religious loses his national excuse for existence. Jehovah expressed it in these words, "Ye shall therefore be holy, for I am holy" (Leviticus 11.45).

The New Testament puts Christians in exactly the same category. Peter calls them "a holy nation" (I Peter 2:9). After declaring the temporal quality of everything else, he presses home the idea that the important thing is holiness. "Seeing then, that all these things shall be dissolved, what manner of persons ought ye to be in all holy conversation and godliness . . ." (II Peter 3:11).

The challenge of the Christian faith is a call to holiness. The man who accepts Jesus Christ as his Saviour takes up this challenge.

JUNE 25   Our actions affect the people we love. If we do well, we bring credit to our parents. If we do badly, to some extent at least, they will be blamed for our actions.

If there is a decent core in a man, he will try desperately to live in such a manner that his life will not reflect poorly upon the people he loves.

The Bible makes mention many times of the fact that we should guard our actions before the world because we are God's people. We are citizens of heaven and should act as such. We are children of the light and should live in the light. We have been born again and should walk in newness of life.

"They shall be mine, saith the Lord of hosts, in that day when I make up my jewels" (Malachi 3:17).

The world sees Jesus Christ in the Christian. If our lives are tarnished by sin of any kind, the unbeliever looks at us and gets a tarnished view of the Saviour.

JUNE 26   Christianity involves a personal choice. There are many mothers who would like to become Christians for their daughters — many fathers who would gladly accept Christ for their sons. But this is impossible because Christianity is the personal business of each individual.

The Psalmist said, "Let thy mercies come also unto me, O Lord, even thy salvation" (Psalm 119:41). Apparently, he knew that his salvation did not depend upon his parents, his friends, or even his religion. It depended upon himself as an individual.

It is easy to settle back on the spirituality of a Christian home and the associations of a Christian church. But these are not enough. There must be a time when you and I — as individuals — choose to commit our lives to God through faith in Christ and say with the Apostle Thomas, "My Lord and my God" (John 20:28).

JUNE 27 No important event in life transpires without deep emotion. Babies are born amid widespread emotion. Lovers are married in a torrent of emotion. Man dies leaving a tidal wave of emotion.

Christianity is intellectually sound but its decisions are made and its battles are fought and its victories are won by emotional forces that go far beyond the power and the ability of the intellect.

The Bible is full of emotion: "The fruit of the Spirit is love, joy, peace" (Galatians 5:22). There is in the human heart a deep well that cannot be filled with the cold logic of reason. It cries out for the warmth of a God-given emotion. Most of our essential needs are emotional and the basis of our fears is to be deprived of these.

In Jesus Christ we can find intellectual stability and emotional security.

JUNE 28 Some of the sting is taken from sin if we think of it as a misfortune. Often we do this; we talk of the unfortunate heathen, the unfortunate criminal, the unfortunate delinquent, the unfortunate drunkard. Each time we use the word we are attempting to protect the sinner from the judgment of God by using a word that puts him in a passive, helpless position instead of an active, responsible one.

The first chapter of Romans makes it quite clear that even the most debauched heathen are not unfortunate heirs of a sinful heritage, but rather personal participants in a sinful life of their own choosing. They had the light of conscience and creation but they chose the darkness of idolatry and superstition.

Jesus did not talk about sin as a passive misfortune but as an active responsibility: "If I had not come and spoken unto them, they had not had sin; but now they have no cloak for their sin" (John 15:22).

JUNE 29 Procrastination is a major deterent to human progress. This is true in business, home, school, and all other forms of activity. Remove this cog and the wheels begin to turn again.

A Greek professor suggested to his class of prospective theologians that they print in large letters on a piece of cardboard the words, "Do It Now!" and hang it over their desks. He believed that this would solve most of their problems in their study of the ancient language.

Procrastination in spiritual matters is one of Satan's most effective weapons. It is not necessary for him to urge us to renounce forever our intentions of getting right with God. All he has to do is put up a sign that says, "Do It Later," and if we heed it, we will be lost.

The Bible says, "Today, if ye will hear his voice, harden not your hearts, as in the provocation" (Hebrews 3:15).

JUNE 30 It is not easy to answer questions about the details of the Bible. Hair-do's, hats, jewelry, eating habits, and marital responsibilities are dealt with in the Bible but create a vast field for discussion when we try to fit them exactly and literally into modern civilization.

There are other more important areas of truth that are presented in the Divine Revelation in a manner that brooks no controversy whatever. The prophet Isaiah may have faced many problems connected with the living habits of God's people, but there was no doubt in his mind about the way of salvation. "Look unto me, and be ye saved, all the ends of the earth: for I am God, and there is none else" (Isaiah 45:22).

It is possible to wander over the winding trails of Biblical detail and miss the main highway to God. Discuss these little problems if you wish, but make sure that your feet are firmly planted on the main road.

JULY 1

In the great, red, double-decked buses of London, England, it is possible to ride quite a distance without paying the fare. Sometimes several city blocks may be traversed before the approaching click and ring of the conductor's box tells you that it is time to pay. The important fact is not when the fare is collected, but that it is collected.

It is true that you may ride with the devil for many years and pay no price for your sin. As a matter of fact you may even prosper and seem to get away with it. However, the Bible declares that some day the fares will be collected, "For evildoers shall be cut off: but those that wait upon the Lord, they shall inherit the earth" (Psalm 37:9).

JULY 2

When a man becomes a Christian he faces the challenge of conflict with the flesh. Before he accepts Christ as his Saviour he is a natural man and nothing more. His entire life is governed by the appetites of the flesh.

The moment he is born again the Holy Spirit enters his life and gives him spiritual life. Now, for the first time, there is a battle raging. The spiritual man and the fleshly man war against each other within the same body. One says, live for yourself. The other urges, live for God.

The Apostle Paul said, "The good that I would I do not: but the evil which I would not, that I do" (Romans 7:19). The battle raged between the flesh and the spirit and it was won only to the degree that Paul yielded himself to the life of the Spirit. The conflict continued but there was always victory through Jesus Christ.

Before conversion there is no spiritual conflict. When we respond to the call of God we enter the field of spiritual military action. If we are not willing to meet the challenge of a battle, we should not become Christians. "No man, having put his hand to the plough, and looking back, is fit for the kingdom of God" (Luke 9:62).

JULY 3

The amount of consistent fellowship that a man has with other believers is a good indication of his love for God and the intensity of his Christianity.

It is inconceivable that a person could live in the same city with people he claimed to love and never go to see them. It is unthinkable that any real Christian could go on living without constant communion with others of like precious faith.

The Bible says, "By this we know that we love the children of God, when we love God" (I John 5:2). The man who does not love the children of God does not love God and the man who has no fellowship with the children of God gives no indication that he really loves them.

JULY 4

Some of the trouble through which we go is the result of natural causes. Jesus made it clear that the eighteen people who were killed when the tower of Siloam fell were no better nor worse than others.

Some trouble is the result of the chastening of the Lord. The Bible says, "Whom the Lord loveth he chasteneth, and scourgeth every son whom he receiveth" (Hebrews 12:6). Only Christians go through this sort of thing. It is a part of the challenge of the life of faith. The reason is expressed in terms of our benefit: "that we might be partakers of His holiness" (Hebrews 12:10).

Some trouble is the result of the direct judgment of God upon sinful man. The Egyptians experienced this in the death of their first born sons when Pharaoh refused to liberate the children of Israel. Uzzah was condemned to death when he touched the ark of God. King Herod was struck down when he made a diabolical speech.

Trouble in the natural course of events is unpleasant. Trouble from the chastening of the Lord is difficult to bear. Trouble from the judgment of God is tragic.

JULY 5

A Christian *is* more than others; he is a child of God. "Wherefore thou art no more a servant, but a son; and if a son, then an heir of God through Christ" (Galatians 4:7).

He *has* more than others; he has access to the grace of God. "My grace is sufficient for thee: for my strength is made perfect in weakness" (II Corinthians 12:9).

He *owes* more than others; he has been redeemed by the blood of Christ. "In whom we have redemption through his blood, even the forgiveness of sins" (Colossians 1:14).

He should *act* more than others. His life should give evidence that he does not belong to Satan. There should be a holy fragrance in his personality that stands in sharp relief against the lack of grace among people of the world.

His character should demonstrate the humility of a slave who realizes that he is the property of God and owes his freedom to the sacrifice of God's Son on the cross.

JULY 6

In our natural state we do not think properly. A man may be quite logical and scientific, his reasoning powers may be of such stature that they dwarf the intellect of others, but in the realm of moral values his mind gives him the wrong answers and leads him in a dangerous direction. Separated from God the human being is a moral idiot who pursues a perilous course.

The Bible declares, "My thoughts are not your thoughts, neither are your ways my ways, saith the Lord" (Isaiah 55:8).

The moral ideas of man are perverted by the curse of sin and the end result of all his actions is wrong. He may do some good things in the course of walking a bad road, but his final destination will be destruction.

Only the power of God can set right our sense of moral and spiritual values and thus reverse our direction. It takes complete regeneration if we are to think God's thoughts and go God's way.

JULY 7   The Bible never promises to take the Christian out of danger but many times it assures him that he will be kept in the midst of it. God did not destroy all of David's enemies, but he looked after him in the midst of them: "Thou preparest a table before me in the presence of mine enemies" (Psalm 23:5).

Safety is a rare commodity in this modern world where little innocent islands as well as big and powerful nations may be trouble spots. The person who has put his faith in Jesus Christ has learned a great secret: Safety does not consist in the absence of danger, but in the presence of the Saviour.

The Bible promises, "When thou liest down, thou shalt not be afraid: yea, thou shalt lie down, and thy sleep shall be sweet. For the Lord shall be thy confidence" (Proverbs 3:24, 26).

JULY 8   Any great religion or political system or philosophy of life must be dogmatic about its basic principles. A man will support something that he believes to be right. If there are not those who are convinced of the justice of a cause to such an extent that they will fight for it, that cause will die.

When one says I am right, then he is also saying, the opposition is wrong. We are being dogmatic about what we believe.

Christianity has rolled across nearly two thousand years of history continually gaining ground because it has held up a dogmatic conviction about the way to God, a conviction that has always declared that all other ways are wrong.

The Bible says, "There is one God, and one mediator between God and men, the man Christ Jesus" (I Timothy 2:5). There is no choice, no alternative, no modification. Only one God and only one way to reach Him. This is dogmatism in its highest form.

JULY 9 Jesus Christ has never forced an entrance to the life of anyone. He is pictured in the Bible as standing on the outside waiting for man to invite Him to come in.

"Behold, I stand at the door, and knock: If any man hear my voice, and open the door, I will come in to him" (Revelation 3:20).

The Son of God will come into our hearts and lives today, but we must ask Him. We must take the initiative. The handle of life's door is on the inside.

Our lives are filled with many things, but we will never be satisfied until we open the door to the Saviour and ask Him to become a part of it all.

JULY 10 It is possible to obey the dictates of your conscience for a lifetime and in the end be hopelessly lost.

There are two kinds of people described in the Bible — good and bad. The good person has a good conscience and the bad person has a bad conscience. A bad conscience is not reliable.

The conscience of an unregenerate man is warped by sin and, rather than showing him the right road, it leads him astray. Such a man never worries about the sinfulness of his actions. Sometimes he may fret about the outcome of his deeds and he mistakenly attributes this fear to the voice of conscience. Fear of punishment and conscience about unrighteousness are two different things.

The conscience of the unbeliever deceives him. The Apostle Paul said, "Sin, taking occasion by the commandment, deceived me" (Romans 7:11). He emphasized the necessity of having a "good conscience" (I Timothy 1:19).

You cannot depend upon your conscience for guidance if you are unsaved. Only when you have been converted can you "let conscience be your guide."

JULY 11 One of the by-products of Christianity is its ability to produce men and women who have good manners. There are few people who ever master all the details of Emily Post, but a good general rule is to be sure that we always act in a manner that is not offensive to other people. The man who does this is a gentleman despite the fact that he may be unlearned in the rules of etiquette.

The Bible frequently reminds the Christian that he should be courteous, kind, and considerate of others. This may only be a reality in the life of one who is in personal contact with God through faith in Christ. Then he possesses the love of God. Paul says, "Charity doth not behave itself unseemly" (I Corinthians 13:5).

The crude people of this world become ladies and gentlemen when they become Christians.

JULY 12 When a man commits his life to God through faith in Christ, for the first time he has peace with God.

Peace involves submission. Before a man is saved he is at enmity with God. When he trusts Christ as his Saviour, he lays down his arms and submits to the rule of God.

Peace involves reconciliation. When Adam sinned the great thing that he lost was fellowship with God. He could no longer walk with God. When a man is saved, the barrier of sin is removed and he has direct access into the presence of God.

The Bible says that Jesus Christ came into the world "that he might reconcile both unto God in one body by the cross, having slain the enmity thereby:

For through him we both have access by one Spirit unto the Father" (Ephesians 2:16-18).

Submission to God and reconciliation with God produce the peace of God.

JULY 13 When it is time to die a man may be in one of two places — in the Lord or outside of the Lord.

Where a man is when he dies depends upon where he lives. It is possible to live in the Lord or to live outside of the Lord.

If he has trusted Jesus Christ as his Saviour, he is living in the Lord and will someday die in the Lord. Otherwise he is outside of the Lord in life and in death.

The Bible holds forth great hope for those who die in the Lord. "Blessed are the dead which die in the Lord from henceforth: Yea, saith the Spirit, that they may rest from their labours; and their works do follow them" (Revelation 14:13).

JULY 14 The city of Berlin was partitioned at the end of World War II but until August of 1961 the gates were left open and the German people could pass freely back and forth between East and West. The East was in the Communist Sector and the West was a part of the "Free World."

There were many differences to be seen by anyone who visited both cities during those years, but one of the most obvious was the lack of light in the East. It may have been caused by many things — no advertising billboards, few automobiles, and a limited number of dull street lights. At any rate the contrast with the brilliantly illuminated city of West Berlin was startling.

The man without Christ lives in a spiritual East Berlin. The Bible describes him as being in the dark. "Ye were sometimes darkness" (Ephesians 5:8). The moment we trust Jesus Christ it is as if we walked into a spiritual West Berlin. "Now are ye light in the Lord" (Ephesians 5:8).

It is important to know that we are living in that sector of the spiritual city where the light has been turned on.

JULY 15 The Second Coming of Christ will end the spiritual opportunity of those who are alive at that time. Some generation of human beings will be living in this world when Jesus Christ comes back again. It may be the next generation. It may be a generation that will live several hundred years from now, or it could be our generation.

The Bible says, "This same Jesus, which is taken up from you into heaven, shall so come in like manner as ye have seen him go into heaven" (Acts 1:11).

No one knows when it will be. The important thing is to be ready whenever it may be, "For in such an hour as ye think not the Son of man cometh" (Matthew 24:44).

JULY 16 The man who does not believe in the Deity of Christ, the resurrection of the dead, the Second Advent, and the final judgment cannot legitimately call himself a Christian.

Accepting one element of the Christian faith — such as the ethics of the Master — does not make a man a Christian. This might be compared to an egg, which is only one of many ingredients in a cake, claiming to be a cake.

A high code of ethics is not peculiar to Christianity. There are many fine moral qualities in Judaism, Mohammedanism and Hinduism, but these are not Christian.

The essential element of Christianity is Jesus Christ, the incarnation of God in human form. The Bible pin-points it in prophetic form in the Old Testament: "Behold God is my salvation; I will trust, and not be afraid; for the Lord, Jehovah is my strength and my song; he also is become my salvation" (Isaiah 12:2).

When Simeon saw Jesus he identified Him with the Old Testament promise — "Mine eyes have seen thy salvation" (Luke 2:30).

JULY 17   Some people reject faith with the slogan, "Seeing is believing." In a more developed form this becomes "proving is believing."

These slogans involve faith in two things — man's powers of sense and his ability to reason. Certainly in this modern world everyone knows that these are far from infallible. Simple instances of optical illusion prove that man cannot believe everything he sees. The very progress of science indicates how many times the reasoning powers of man have given him the wrong answers and they have had to be changed.

The Christian declares his faith in Jesus Christ and the Word of God calls him blessed. "Blessed are they that have not seen, and yet have believed" (John 20:29).

JULY 18   There are two kinds of religious skeptics. One is professional and the other is honest.

The professional skeptic is usually motivated by the hope of financial returns. He is the man whose articles appear in magazines and newspapers. Often he does not really believe what he says. He is just a rather mixed-up little boy who is trying to keep the bread and butter on his table at the expense of some other person's faith.

The honest skeptic is confronted with intellectual problems that he would like to solve. He has legitimate questions to which he wants to find answers. He may be somewhat naive in his approach but he is at least honest in his search for the truth.

In either case the skeptic attempts to reason his way from his own little material world to God. The Bible suggests that he turn around and start with God and then let the rest of the universe fall into place. "The fear of the Lord is the beginning of wisdom: a good understanding have all they that do his commandments" (Psalm 111:10).

JULY 19 It is a good thing to pray but it will not do any good unless you are a Christian. Hundreds of people cannot understand why God does not answer their prayers. The reason is that God has not promised to answer everyone's prayers.

Prayer is an extremely limited privilege always guarded by conditions. It does not matter how fervently a man may pray or how often, if he is not a righteous man God is not obligated to hear him. The Bible says, "The effectual fervent prayer of a righteous man availeth much"(James 5:16).

Better not to waste your time praying until you have put yourself by faith into the class of people to whom God has obligated Himself. Trust Christ as your Saviour, live for God, and be a righteous man; then the promise is for you.

JULY 20 Sometimes the voice of God is heard through signs.

The classic example in the Bible is the story of Gideon and his fleece: "Behold, I will put a fleece of wool in the floor; and if the dew be on the fleece only, and it be dry upon all the earth beside, then shall I know that thou wilt save Israel by mine hand" (Judges 6:37).

Gideon accepted the results of this test as the voice of God assuring him that he should lead the people against their enemies.

This is a fascinating story but the same sort of thing may never happen to us. Some of us will never experience a miraculous sign such as this. However, God has not left us without His specific instructions. His voice is continued in the Book which we call the Bible. When the Bible speaks, God speaks.

Listen to the voice of God as He speaks to the transgressor: "I, even I, am he that blotteth out thy transgressions for mine own sake, and will not remember thy sins" (Isaiah 43:25).

JULY 21 Something always happens when the Word of God is heard. It never hangs idle in the air waves as does man's word; it constantly acts either in salvation or judgment.

Thousands have been saved when they have heard the Word of God — saved because they have responded to it and obeyed it. Thousands stand condemned by the same Word because they have neglected it or rebelled against it.

The Bible says, "So shall my word be that goeth forth out of my mouth: it shall not return unto me void, but it shall accomplish that which I please" (Isaiah 55:11).

The same water that buoyed up the ark and saved Noah drowned the people who had not gone in. The same death angel that slew the Egyptians saved the Israelites. The same Word that results in salvation to those who accept it will stand in judgment upon those who reject it.

JULY 22 The rich young ruler knew all the answers. When Jesus questioned him about the commandments he said that he had observed them since he was a boy. Probably he had been reared in a religious family and knew the language of faith, but despite his intellectual assent to an orthodox creed, the Bible portrays him asking the question, "Good Master, what shall I do that I may inherit eternal life?" (Mark 10:17).

In this case his head told him he was right but his heart told him he was wrong. His head gave him confidence but his heart brought him under conviction. He had all the answers, but no assurance. He had intellect without experience.

People like the rich young ruler attend every evangelical church. They know the language, observe the customs, and go through the motions of Christianity without ever having come to the place of conviction and repentance and salvation through personal faith in Christ.

JULY 23   The rich farmer prepared for the needs of his physical being but neglected his soul. He said to himself, "Take thine ease, eat, drink, and be merry" (Luke 12:19), and he laid away a store of food and wine sufficient to satisfy all the material needs he would ever have.

God called him a fool because he ignored the real man that would go on living after his body had died. He neglected to provide for the part of him that could not be fed with grain and fruit.

Jesus told His disciples about bread and water that was spiritual. "I am the bread of life; he that cometh to me shall never hunger; and he that believeth on me shall never thirst" (John 6:35).

JULY 24   It is possible for a man to have had everything and to have done everything and then conclude that life is empty. The preacher in Ecclesiastes was such a man. He was the son of a king and there was no material or physical desire of his that had not been consummated. As he commented on the world he had enjoyed to the full he said, "Vanity of vanities; all is vanity. What profit hath a man of all his labour which he taketh under the sun?" (Ecclesiastes 1:2, 3).

In much the same situation, another group of people floundered about helplessly looking for an answer to their needs and God sent a prophet with a simple answer, "Consider your ways" (Haggai 1:5), and turn to the House of God.

The answer of the Bible for a boring life is not physical, but spiritual. It is spiritual hunger that produces the pangs of emptiness and nothing material will ever satisfy it. Only a personal union with Jesus Christ can supply the antidote for material monotony.

JULY 25

When we are in love we are usually enthusiastic about the object of our love. Everything we do and say is colored to some extent by it. It is a calamity on the human level when we lose the intense enthusiasm of our early love for one another.

In the spiritual realm it is a blessing to meet a man who is just as enthusiastic about the Lord at fifty as he was at fifteen. It is a mark of spiritual deterioration when this characteristic of our love for God is gone.

Jesus said, "Thou shalt love the Lord thy God with all thy heart, and with all thy soul, and with all thy mind" (Matthew 22:37).

JULY 26

There are immeasurable advantages in a Christian home. It should be a stepping stone that leads to God. In some cases, however, it may be a stumbling block of embarrassment that keeps us away from God.

In every good church there are young people who know the way of salvation and who sense their own deep need of forgiveness, but whenever the opportunity of decision is given they are too embarrassed to respond.

"Mother is a godly woman and she thinks I am a Christian. Father is an elder and he takes it for granted that I am right with God. If I raise my hand, walk the aisle, or kneel at the altar, what will my parents think?"

And so they wait — good young people, well versed in the Bible, conscious of their own need, but allowing a Christian home to be the stumbling block that embarrasses them slowly toward hell.

Perhaps the Apostle was thinking of these when he wrote to Corinth with a note of great urgency: "We are ambassadors for Christ, as though God did beseech you by us: we pray you in Christ's stead, be ye reconciled to God" (II Corinthians 5:20).

JULY 27 The Divine Benefactor of the Twenty-third Psalm becomes the Chief Judge of the New Testament. The Bible says, "And when the chief Shepherd shall appear, ye shall receive a crown of glory that fadeth not away" (I Peter 5:4).

This is a blessed consolation to the Christian but it is a sobering thought to the person who will not share in the reward. It is obvious that if there are those who will be rewarded there must also be others who will not; but the Word of God does not leave us with nothing more than this human assumption, "Tribulation and anguish, upon every soul of man that doeth evil . . . But glory, honour, and peace, to every man that worketh good" (Romans 2:9, 10).

If we know Jesus Christ as the Good Shepherd now we can look forward to the crown from the hand of the Chief Shepherd on the Day of Judgment.

JULY 28 The work of the church is not to Christianize the world but to evangelize it.

Christianization implies a world in which everyone has become a Christian. If this is the task of the Church, she has failed miserably. After two thousand years of church history there are more non-Christians than there were during the days of the Apostles. Unsaved people are being born much faster than converts are being made.

The Bible does not present the objective as Christianization but evangelization — a worldwide preaching of the Gospel in such a manner that all have an adequate opportunity of accepting it and becoming Christians. "God at the first did visit the Gentiles to take out of them a people for his name" (Acts 15:14).

The Church consists of those who have heard the Gospel and have responded to the call of the Spirit and God. When the last one is called the Church will be complete and Christ will return.

JULY 29 There are many roads that lead from God but there is only one road that leads to God. Every form of sin takes man away from God. He may be a murderer or a liar, an idolator or a thief. He may have an unclean mind or a proud heart. He may choose any one of a great many paths that combine to form the broad way that ends in destruction.

When we realize that we are headed in the wrong direction we discover that there is only one straight and narrow way that leads back to God. Jesus made it very clear that He is the Way. When we accept Jesus Christ by faith we are entering by way of Christ into a personal relationship with God.

When Paul and Silas preached in Philippi urging men and women to turn to Christ, a demon-inspired girl realized what some of the normal people had not realized. She cried out, "These men are the servants of the most high God, which show unto us the way of salvation" (Acts 16:17).

JULY 30 There are two standards of good. There is the standard of man and the standard of God. Many people may be termed good as far as the world is concerned. This usually means that a man is as good as most others and better than some.

God's standard of good is quite different and the only One who has ever measured up to it is Jesus Christ. When a person is dealing with God he must meet God's conditions and no mere man that has ever lived has been able to do so. This means that if any man is to be acceptable in God's sight, he must be clothed in the goodness of God's Son, Jesus Christ. This happens when a man makes vital contact with God through faith in Christ.

The Apostle Paul described it in these words, "And be found in him, not having mine own righteousness . . . but that which is through the faith of Christ" (Philippians 3:9).

JULY 31 Only the very naive would attempt to take the idea of hell out of the Christian religion. Any creed that omits hell may be a lofty one, but it falls short of being Christian.

It is difficult to understand all that hell involves. It may be nothing more than perpetual physical torment. It may be a never-ending existence in a world of harrassing memories. It may be a constant agony of dying, or it may be a combination of these and more.

Whatever else may be implied, one fact stands out: Hell is separation from God and from everything and everyone that is good. When Jesus told the story of the rich man and Lazarus, he described the rich man in a place of punishment and Lazarus "afar off" with Abraham.

The Bible speaks about God "Taking vengeance on them that know not God, and that obey not the gospel of our Lord Jesus Christ: Who shall be punished with everlasting destruction from the presence of the Lord, and from the glory of his power" (II Thessalonians 1:8-9).

Failure to respond to the Bible means judgment and judgment involves separation.

AUG. 1

It is important that we know Jesus Christ now, because our resurrection unto everlasting life depends upon whether or not our spiritual ears respond to His voice. In John's gospel Jesus said that one of the characteristics of His sheep is that they know and obey His voice. This is the miracle that will call the dead in Christ from their graves.

Jesus said, "The hour is coming when the dead shall hear the voice of the Son of God: and they that hear shall live. For as the Father hath life in himself; so hath he given to the Son to have life in himself" (John 5:25-26).

Most people have their ears tuned to the sounds of the world, but the ears of their souls are deaf to the voice of God and the sounds of the spiritual universe. The sounds of the world cannot reach the dead, but the voice of God can.

AUG. 2

Sin would not be so repulsive if we were to look upon it as mistaken judgment. Man is continually called upon to make decisions, to choose his direction. He cannot be right all the time and in every situation. When he makes the wrong decision, he has sinned.

This takes the barb out of sin but of course it is not true to the Bible's description. James describes the sinner as a man who deliberately goes the wrong way despite the fact that he knows better, "Therefore to him that knoweth to do good, and doeth it not, to him it is sin" (I Peter 2:24).

The Bible undoubtedly indicates that we are born in sin, but apart from this entirely, it describes all men as deliberate, active sinners by their own choice.

The power of the Gospel is such that not only helpless humanity may be saved but that headstrong humanity may be rescued as well. The Bible says that Jesus Christ "bare our sins in his own body on the tree, that we, being dead to sins, should live unto righteousness" (James 4:17).

AUG. 3 "Drink no longer water, but use a little wine for thy stomach's sake and thine often infirmities" (I Timothy 5:23). This was Paul's advice to Timothy.

The Bible tells men to stop drinking water, if the water is making them sick, and take a little wine as a medicine.

This is the only verse in the Bible that recommends alcohol for any purpose and here, it is obviously to be taken like any other medicine — by the spoonful.

From Genesis through Revelation, the Bible discourages the consumption of alcohol as a beverage. It warns men of its devastating effects and includes the drunkard among those who must finally be lost eternally.

To all sinners the Word of God offers a drink that will remove permanently the need of any alcoholic stimulation. "And let him that is athirst come. And whosoever will, let him take the water of life freely" (Revelation 22:17).

AUG. 4 There are three levels of knowledge — the beginner, the student, and the scholar.

The beginner sees only the problem; he does not know why it exists or how it may be solved. All he can do is ask questions. The student has advanced to the stage where he not only sees the problem but also knows its causes. The scholar has matured intellectually to the extent that he knows some of the answers.

Many questions about the Bible without reasons or answers is a sign of a childish mind spiritually. Problems based on logical grounds but without adequate solutions indicate a juvenile spiritual understanding. Difficulties with a satisfactory number of logical answers and faith in God for those that are unanswered reveals maturity.

This is within easy reach of anyone. The Bible says, "If any of you lack wisdom, let him ask of God; that giveth to all men liberally" (James 1:5).

AUG. 5

Whenever Jesus saw hungry people, He was moved with compassion and at least twice it is recorded in the Bible that He actually fed them. However, it was quite evident that His greatest mission on earth was to help people spiritually. He spoke of spiritual water that would quench a spiritual thirst and spiritual bread that would satisfy a spiritual hunger.

In His first great sermon He declared His concern for the part of man that is not physical when He said, "Blessed are they which do hunger and thirst after righteousness: for they shall be filled" (Matthew 5:6).

The hunger for righteousness is a universal need and it is never met until the life is committed to God by faith in Christ and the Divine miracle of the new birth takes place.

AUG. 6

There is always an end to the mercy of man. The law courts may be merciful but only within prescribed limits. Some individuals have a great capacity for mercy but there is a point beyond which they cannot go.

If the Bible were to describe God with a degree of mercy much more expansive than man's but limited in some manner, we could easily grasp it. If we knew that there was a depth of sin which man could reach and never have any hope of being forgiven because God's mercy had been exhausted, we could understand it. This would be a human method of government. This is what we would do and what we would expect God to do. Our limited sense of right and wrong tells us that there should be a point of no return.

It is with considerable bewilderment that we pick up the Divine Library and learn that such is not the case. In this life there is no "point of no return" with God. There is no limit to His mercy. It has never been exhausted. "Praise ye the Lord. O give thanks unto the Lord; for he is good: for his mercy endureth for ever" (Psalm 106:1).

AUG. 7 The Bible describes the Christian as a "peculiar" person. This does not mean that he should look odd or act in a ridiculous manner. It does mean that he is set apart as a servant of God. He is God's special property and therefore he is different from other people. He is a marked man.

He is peculiar because he is going in the opposite direction to the people around him. They are going down stream with the crowd to please themselves. The Christian has repented. He has turned around and now he is going up stream, against the crowd, to please God.

The Bible says because you are "a peculiar people . . . ye should shew forth the praises of him who hath called you out of darkness into his marvellous light" (I Peter 2:9).

AUG. 8 As long as we compare ourselves with other people we will not be convicted of our own sin. Usually we can say that we are as good as most people and better than some. Each of us has his good qualities and his bad and apart from a few who are exceptionally righteous and a few who are extremely wicked, the rest of us level off at a common denominator of goodness.

It was only when the good men in the Bible compared themselves with God that they realized how evil they really were. Isaiah was one of the best men of his generation, but when he saw the holiness of God he became aware of his own human depravity. "Then said I, Woe is me! for I am undone; because I am a man of unclean lips, and I dwell in the midst of a people of unclean lips: for mine eyes have seen the King, the Lord of hosts" (Isaiah 6:5).

When a man lifts his eyes beyond the apparent goodness of man to the obvious holiness of God, he is convinced of his own desperate need and cries out for the help that only Jesus Christ can give.

AUG. 9   In the Japanese language there is no word for sin. The nearest word to it is "crime."

This is not an accurate definition, of course, because a crime is an offense against our fellow men. Sin is an offense against God and is a much more serious thing. The Japanese Evangelist may get the Bible idea across by translating the word "sin" as a "crime against the true and living God."

The Bible explains it in these words, "Whosoever committeth sin transgresseth also the law: for sin is the transgression of the law" (I John 3:4).

The "law" in this context is not the law of the land, but rather the law of God.

The sinner is confronted with the prospect of standing as a transgressor before the holy Law Giver. If he stands alone, he is condemned. If he stands in Christ, he is saved.

AUG. 10   The only really reliable witness is an eyewitness. The proof of an experience is to have it. I cannot adequately compare any two countries unless I have lived in both. I cannot state the relative value of two conditions unless I am familiar with both.

No one knows the value of being a Christian until he is one. Others make comparisons but they cannot possibly know what they are talking about. The sinner is in no position to say whether being in the world or in Christ brings the greater happiness. He is not an authority on the subject because he knows only one side of it.

An automobile manufacturer uses the slogan, "Ask the man who owns one." Jesus used exactly the same argument when He talked to Nicodemus and said, "We speak that we do know, and testify that we have seen" (John 3:11).

If you want a reliable testimony about Christianity, ask an eye-witness, a man who can say: "I have trusted, I have seen, and I have found."

AUG. 11   It is possible to have a great outward show of religion without having any inward evidence of spirituality. The Bible says, "They come unto thee as the people cometh, and they sit before thee as my people, and they hear thy words, but they will not do them: for with their mouth they show much love, but their heart goeth after covetousness" (Ezekiel 33:31).

Many people love their local church. They enjoy singing the songs and hymns of the Christian faith. They have an average knowledge of the Bible and read it occasionally. They would never think of sleeping without praying first, but they have never had a spiritual experience with God. They have never repented of their sin and asked the Lord to save them. "The sacrifices of God are a broken spirit: a broken and a contrite heart, O God, thou wilt not despise" (Psalm 51:17).

AUG. 12   The test of Christianity is not what we have received but how much we have given.

In the back of the worldly man's mind is the question: "What do I get out of it?" He lives his life for himself. He is an egomaniac. He may successfully camouflage his motive, but it is always there in his subconscious mind if not in the forefront of his thinking.

When a man becomes a child of God his motive undergoes a transformation. He begins to live for others. The question of his life is: "What can I put into it?" or "How will this help other people?"

The Bible says, "Look not every man on his own things, but every man also on the things of others" (Philippians 2:4). Translated into his life the Apostle Paul testified, "Even as I please all men in all things, not seeking mine own profit but the profit of many, that they may be saved" (I Corinthians 10:33).

Only the grace of God in a human heart could produce this kind of unselfishness.

AUG.
13

There are advantages in living a good life despite the fact that it has no power to save a man. Any degree to which we can avoid sin during our early years will spare us from many sorrows and regrets in later life.

By living righteously we may never be confronted by a strong habit that we cannot break or be associated with the kind of friends who are a hindrance to us. We may refrain from doing something in youth for which we will hate ourselves in old age.

However, the Bible makes it clear that salvation does not come at the end of the good life, but at the moment we trust Christ for it: "If thou shalt confess with thy mouth the Lord Jesus, and shalt believe in thine heart that God hath raised him from the dead, thou shalt be saved" (Romans 10:9).

AUG.
14

The Bible advocated the power of positive thinking nearly two thousand years before modern psychologists discovered it. Within the last few years dozens of books have been written on the subject and have become best-sellers.

Modern authors are aware of the unlimited potential of positive thought but most of them fail to tell us where to find this power. This is where the Bible proves itself superior to the works of man. It locates the power of positive thinking in love: "Charity thinketh no evil" (I John 4:8). And it traces love directly to God: "He that loveth not knoweth not God; for God is love" (I Corinthians 13:5).

Positive thinking starts with God, who is love. When we commit our lives to Him a miracle takes place that makes us the recipients of God's love. The Bible declares that love thinks right.

Once you reach this point the books on positive thinking are valuable. Without personal contact with God a thousand volumes on positive thinking are absolutely useless.

AUG. 15 A man may respect religion without having any. There are those who never go to church themselves but would rebel against the idea of doing away with all the churches in their town, and if a member of their family were to be married or buried, they would insist upon a minister and a service.

These are the people who would get out and vote for prohibition and buy bootleg liquor, give a big gift to the Community Chest and underpay their own employees, or talk about racial tolerance and bar a colored man from their club.

The Bible describes them: "They profess that they know God; but in works they deny him, being abominable, and disobedient, and unto every good work reprobate" (Titus 1:16).

A nominal respect for religion will not stand up before God. He insists upon a life that has been committed completely to Him through faith in Jesus Christ.

AUG. 16 Almost everyone can remember his first days at school. The teacher said that in 1492 Columbus landed in the West Indies. Undoubtedly everyone believes the story, but no one in this generation was actually there when it happened.

This is one of the many facts of history that are accepted by faith. As a matter of fact, most education is dependent upon faith —faith in a man's word, faith in a book, faith in the label on a bottle.

The Bible declares that religion is a matter of faith. Contact with God involves faith. Remove the element of faith from any system of thought and man is left with a philosophy or a psychology of life but without any religion whatsoever.

The Bible declares that all the great spiritual leaders were men of faith, "Who through faith subdued kingdoms, wrought righteousness, obtained promises, stopped the mouths of lions" (Hebrews 11:33).

AUG. 17

The Bible talks about people who have an extremely high I.Q. in sin but are moronical in righteousness. They know all the angles, the shortcuts, the joints, and the fast talk. In the language of the world, "they've been around," but when confronted with the important things of life they are the personification of stupidity.

They know how to place a bet but they do not know how to get to heaven. They know how to sin but they know nothing about being good. They can tell dirty jokes to a dirty friend but they would not be able to help him get right with God if he were dying.

Jeremiah said, "For my people is foolish, they have not known me; they are sottish children, and they have none understanding: they are wise to do evil, but to do good they have no knowledge" (Jeremiah 4:22).

You can test your own I.Q. by the standards of the Bible.

AUG. 18

A Christian's life is never ended until his work is finished.

At one time in Jerusalem it looked as if the end had come for the Apostle Paul. The people wanted to kill him and it was only the fact that he was a Roman citizen that saved him.

It was in the midst of this crisis that the Lord spoke to Paul and assured him that his work was not yet done. "Be of good cheer, Paul: for as thou hast testified of me in Jerusalem, so must thou bear witness also at Rome" (Acts 23:11).

It is a source of comfort for the Christian to know that his life is in the hands of God and that he will be spared to do the task for which God has called him.

It is vitally important that we use carefully the years that God gives us and that we spend our days doing the thing to which He has called us.

AUG. 19

There is little virtue in trying to live a Christian life until a man becomes a Christian. The Apostle Paul tells the Corinthians that even martyrdom is of no value unless it involves a child of God who gives his life for God. "Though I give my body to be burned, and have not charity, it profiteth me nothing" (I Corinthians 13:3).

Of course, *charity* here means love, and the only person who knows anything about real love is the one who knows God. The Bible says, "We have known and believed the love that God hath to us. God is love; and he that dwelleth in love dwelleth in God, and God in him" (I John 4:16).

It is more important to know God than to be a martyr and it is useless to be a martyr if you do not know God.

AUG. 20

In the process of living man is continually dying. Every time we draw breath we prolong life; this is inspiration. Each time breath leaves us we are dying; this is expiration. Some day we will breathe out for the final time and our friends will say we have expired.

When God created Adam the Bible says, "The Lord God formed man of the dust of the ground, and breathed into his nostrils the breath of life; and man became a living soul" (Genesis 2:7).

Man should have lived forever and death should have been a complete stranger to him, but sin broke the silver cord of life and now man expires. He dies — perhaps at an early age or in the prime of life or during the twilight years — but inevitably death waits at the end of the human road.

The Gospel is the good news that through simple faith in Christ we can regain what was lost in the Garden of Eden. Jesus said, "I am the resurrection, and the life: he that believeth in me, though he were dead, yet shall he live" (John 11:25).

The inspiration of faith generates a life that will never expire.

AUG. 21   Real faith demands action. A man may believe in the effectiveness of the light switch to bring about the illumination of a room, but until he turns the switch the room remains in darkness.

Thousands of lost souls have lived with the switch of faith at their fingertips. They know where it is. They know what it will do, but they grope in spiritual darkness because some form of sin paralyzes the hand that would turn on the light of the Gospel.

That is why the salvation verses of the Bible contain so many verbs of action. "Come; for all things are now ready. . . . Take my yoke upon you. . . . He that eateth of this bread shall live forever. . . . If any man thirst, let him come unto me and drink" (Luke 14:17, Matthew 11:29, John 6:58; 7:37). There is no salvation apart from an active step of faith.

AUG. 22   Sometimes it is suggested that we should live for today and for this life and we should not concern ourselves about the next life.

This is easy to say but impossible to do. Man cannot help but think about eternity. If we were not reminded of death so constantly, we might be able to concentrate only upon this world.

But death is with us always, stalking the pages of our newspapers, interrupting the beauty of our country-side, and making great marble monuments in the midst of our cities. In a world that is harrassed by death, we must have hope beyond it. We must know that we are ready for the next world; otherwise we are unhappy.

The Bible says, "If in this life only we have hope in Christ, we are of all men most miserable. But now is Christ risen from the dead, and become the first fruits of them that slept" (I Corinthians 15:19, 20).

AUG.
23
Becoming a Christian involves an exclusive choice. It is not a synthesis of the valuable elements of several different ways of life. It is not a union of the other great religious beliefs. It is not an amalgamation of many gods into a monotheistic form.

When Elijah confronted the children of Israel with the claims of Baal, he might have suggested a union of Baal and Jehovah to form an ecumenical faith more powerful than any the world had ever known. Instead of a union he demanded a choice. "How long halt ye between two opinions? If the Lord be God, follow him: but if Baal, then follow him" (I Kings 18:21).

The Bible presents an exclusive religion, not a sentimental synthesis of paganism and Christianity. The man who is a child of God has made an exclusive choice to commit his life to God through faith in Christ.

AUG.
24
Sin is the conscious willful choice of evil and has in it a certain maliciousness against God which is far worse than crime, mistaken judgment, misfortune, or insanity.

The devil would have us camouflage sin by calling it many different names that excuse man of his own part in it and describe him as a sort of pathetic passive pawn in a game over which he has no control. Sin often does include all of these other elements, but they are only a part, one aspect, of sin.

It is the intrinsic diabolical wickedness of sin that demands a supernatural Saviour and it is the miracle that saved man from his sin that leads the saints in heaven to look back upon their lives and sing: "Thou art worthy to take the book, and to open the seals thereof: for thou wast slain, and hast redeemed us to God by thy blood out of every kindred, and tongue, and people, and nation" (Revelation 5:9).

AUG. 25

Many people claim to be searching for the truth. Some are quite honest in their quest and prove it by their willingness to accept the truth when they find it.

Others are professional agnostics and they prove it by refusing to accept the truth when they do see it. These people try all the churches and all the systems of thought and never arrive at any conclusions.

When the Apostle Paul wrote to Timothy he described the last days as a period when a wicked generation would claim to be religious and intelligent, but he portrays them as "Ever learning, and never able to come to the knowledge of the truth" (II Timothy 3:7).

In simple language Jesus solved the problem of man's search for truth by saying, "I am the truth . . . no man cometh unto the Father, but by me" (John 14:6).

AUG. 26

The Bible pictures Jesus as a Saviour whose heart is filled with compassion when He sees the needs of others. "When he saw the multitudes, he was moved with compassion on them, because they fainted, and were scattered abroad, as sheep having no shepherd" (Matthew 9:36).

It is a false conception of Christ if we do not consider the complete picture. The Bible also presents Jesus as a holy Judge whose righteousness condemns the unrepentant sinner to eternal doom. "Then shall he say also unto them on the left hand, Depart from me, ye cursed, into everlasting fire, prepared for the devil and his angels" (Matthew 25:41). Matthew 25:41).

This is the day of compassion. The arms are outstretched, the door is open, and the invitation is to the whole world. Tomorrow may inaugurate the day of condemnation when the finger of judgment will be pointed, the door closed, and the invitation ended.

AUG. 27 A good doctor should know his patient and be able to diagnose his case. The diagnosis is of little value unless he can also suggest a remedy that will bring results.

Jesus referred to Himself as a physician: "They that be whole need not a physician, but they that are sick" (Matthew 9:12). It is true that He helped many people in a literal physical sense, but in this verse He was talking about His mission to the world as that of a spiritual physician — One who can satisfy the need in the life of a man who may be perfectly well physically.

Christians who have felt His power sing about Him as "The Great Physician." He knows the heart of every man and He has diagnosed the trouble as sin. He is able to point out the remedy — a complete committal of life to Him forever, and the remedy always works.

AUG. 28 It is dangerous to base any important belief on an isolated passage of Scripture or one verse taken out of its setting in the Bible.

The false cults of the world lure Christians into their assemblies by using the Bible as a text book, but inevitably their beliefs are based upon verses used entirely out of context and not at all in accordance with the teaching of the whole Bible.

When Jesus taught He did so from a knowledge of all the Old Testament Scriptures, "Beginning at Moses and all the prophets, he expounded unto them in all the scriptures the things concerning himself" (Matthew 24:27). His claims to Deity and Messiahship were not taken from scattered passages but from the teaching of the complete Jewish Bible.

The Bible says, "Beloved, believe not every spirit, but try the spirits whether they are of God" (I John 4:1). One good way to do this is to make sure that your beliefs are in line with the teaching of the entire Bible.

AUG. 29 There are some people who are conscious of their sin and would welcome the truth that would lead them to deliverance. Usually they look in the wrong places — books, speeches, organizations, and philosophies. At the end of their search they are more perplexed than ever but still aware of their need.

The best place to find help is in the Word of God. The sincere seeker will find that as he reads the Bible the Spirit of God will cause the truth to enter his soul and bring him to salvation.

The Psalmist asked the question, "Wherewithal shall a young man cleanse his way?" Then he answered his own question: "By taking heed thereto according to thy word" (Psalm 119:9).

There is a miraculous power in the Word of God that can change a man's life. This may be said of no other book.

AUG. 30 If a man is a Christian, it should be evident to the rest of the world. When the light is turned on in a dark room it is obvious. If a corpse were to rise from its coffin and live again, there would be no need to hang a sign about the neck to tell the world there had been a change. When the doors of a penitentiary swing outward and a prisoner walks into freedom, it is immediately apparent.

The Bible tells the story of the early Christians in these words, "When they saw the boldness of Peter and John . . . they marvelled; and they took knowledge of them, that they had been with Jesus" (Acts 4:13).

The lives of these two had been changed by the power of God from darkness to light, from death to life, from bondage to freedom, and everyone with whom they came into contact knew it.

If a man's birth is not evident to his friends, it may be that he has never really trusted Jesus Christ as his Saviour and is still a stranger to redemption.

AUG. 31 The man who is not a Christian bases his life upon the opinions of the world. He leans heavily upon the people and the books of the world. The Bible describes him as one who walks "in the counsel of the ungodly" (Psalm 1:1).

Not only does he gain his opinions from the world but he stands where the man of the world stands as far as his actions are concerned: he "standeth in the way of sinners" (Psalm 1:1).

If he continues to ignore the claims of Christ he will not only be godless himself but he will sit in the chair of agnosticism in the University of Satan: he "sitteth in the seat of the scornful" (Psalm 1:1).

This is always the course of sin. It is thought, then practiced, and finally taught.

The man who trusts Christ as his Saviour learns his basic principles of life from the Bible and judges the opinions of other men and books in accordance with the Word of God — "But his delight is in the law of the Lord; and in his law doth he meditate day and night" (Psalm 1:2).

SEPT. 1 Some people are afraid to go to church because they might get saved and they think that is the last thing in the world that they would want to happen to them.

The Bible says, "Every one that doeth evil hateth the light, neither cometh to the light, lest his deeds should be reproved" (John 3:20). Some people actually love their sin so much that they hate anything that might take it away from them.

When a person goes to church he hears the Word of God. He is convicted of his sin and conviction sometimes results in repentance and repentance leads to salvation.

The average sinner will use every excuse imaginable to keep away from a gospel service and he will blame everyone but himself. Usually, he does not go because he thinks he prefers his sin to salvation.

SEPT. 2 Man's relationship to Jesus Christ determines his present state. If he has trusted Christ he is already in possession of eternal life. He does not look forward to it. He has it.

If he has not trusted Christ, he does not have eternal life and he already lives under the shadow of the wrath of God. The Bible says, "He that believeth on the Son hath everlasting life: and he that believeth not the Son shall not see life; but the wrath of God abideth on him" (John 3:36).

We have difficulty picturing the wrath of God. We are tragically familiar with the wrath of man. We have seen it demonstrated in all of its insidious forms of brutality and sadism. The only good thing about the wrath of man is that it must end with death.

Think of the wrath of man in its most extreme form and then multiply your picture by infinity and you may have some hazy conception of what it will mean to reject Jesus Christ and exist forever under the wrath of God.

SEPT. 3 A Christian is a man who has been born twice. He must be born the first time physically or he would not be in existence at all. He must be born the second time spiritually or he cannot be a part of the Kingdom of God.

No one really understands the principle of life that brings a human being into existence. But we accept the fact despite our appalling lack of knowledge about it. No one can comprehend the magnitude of spiritual birth, but the Bible tells us it is necessary and explains that the way to bring it about is to trust the Son of God as Saviour. The human part we can do; the miracle of spiritual life we must leave to God.

Jesus said to Nicodemus, "Except a man be born of water and of the Spirit, he cannot enter into the kingdom of God" (John 3:5).

SEPT. 4 The Old Testament is filled with the sacrifices of animals but not one of these sacrifices was able to take away sin. As each animal's blood was shed, the people looked forward in faith to the time when God would send into the world His own Son to die and become the supreme sacrifice for all sin.

The Bible says, "It is not possible that the blood of bulls and of goats should take away sins" (Hebrews 10:4). These were necessary, but simply symbols of the great sacrifice of Christ on the cross.

It was this to which John the Baptist looked forward when he announced the arrival of Jesus at the Jordan River, "Behold, the Lamb of God which taketh away the sin of the world" (John 1:29).

The day these words were first spoken there were those who turned from their sin and looked to Christ for salvation. A man becomes a child of God the moment he looks in faith toward Calvary and allows Jesus Christ to become his supreme sacrifice.

SEPT. 5   Everyone is the slave of some master. One serves fortune, another is chained to fame and a third is the victim of fashion.

The Bible declares that it is possible for man to serve sin or else he may be freed from sin by grace and obey God. "Being then made free from sin, ye became the servants of righteousness" (Romans 6:18).

The book of Romans reminds us that the service of sin brings shame and spiritual death, but the grace of God through Jesus Christ gives eternal life. "What fruit had ye then in those things whereof ye are now ashamed? For the end of those things is death. But now being made free from sin and become servants to God ye have your fruit unto holiness, and the end everlasting life" (Romans 6:21, 22).

SEPT. 6   A man does not look for the way home until he realizes that he is lost. He does not consider his need of a doctor until he is sick. He will never trust the Saviour until he is conscious of his own spiritual helplessness.

The Bible says, "All we like sheep have gone astray" (Isaiah 53:6). This is a sweeping statement with no limitations. It includes everyone under the same indictment — away from God.

Then it says, "We have turned everyone to his own way" (Isaiah 53:6). This places the responsibility for sin on our own doorstep. This verse declares that in our lifetime we have done what Adam did in his. We have deliberately gone our way rather than God's.

Finally, the verse points the way to salvation, "And the Lord hath laid upon him the iniquity of us all." We were lost because we had sinned, but Christ died to pay the penalty that should have been ours. When we trust Him as our Saviour we are accepting His payment as complete and final.

SEPT. 7 The Christian who claims to believe in God but refuses to accept the doctrine of punishment for sin in the next life, would be something like a Japanese who claimed to believe in Shintoism but refused to accept the worship of his ancestors.

When any man gives up the major doctrines of his religion he is no longer an adherent of that religion.

The self-styled Christian who denies the existence of sin and the possibility of punishment may continue to be a very religious man but it would constitute sheer ignorance for him to profess Christianity.

Listen to the words of Jesus, "Many will say to me in that day, Lord, Lord, have we not prophesied in thy name? And then will I profess unto them, I never knew you: depart from me, ye that work iniquity" (Matthew 7:22-23).

SEPT. 8 The ethics of Jesus Christ do not result in our redemption. No other religious leader ever lived an absolutely blameless life. The Man of Galilee stands alone in this respect and when we are looking for a model by which to pattern our lives His is the highest.

He taught the world the significance of giving to help others and as a result every drive to raise money for humanitarian purposes stems from the principles He established.

But the Bible never associates ethics or giving with redemption. From Genesis through Revelation the only way of redemption is the shedding of blood. Before the cross the atonement was made in type with the blood of animals. After the cross the Bible looks back to that sacrifice as the supreme atonement of the Lamb of God.

The Bible says, "Ye were not redeemed with corruptible things, as silver and gold . . . But with the precious blood of Christ, as of a lamb without blemish and without spot" (I Peter 1:18, 19).

SEPT.
9
In a truly Christian home the wall of family worship has been built. It is difficult to keep the family unit together in these times, but reading the Bible and praying with the family will make it a great deal easier.

The basic principles of the Word of God are the guide to Christian living and the major spiritual deterrent to unrighteousness. "All scripture is given by inspiration of God, and is profitable for doctrine, for reproof, for correction, for instruction in righteousness" (II Timothy 3:16).

The Psalmist refers to the Bible as a lamp. What a tragedy it would be to try and rear children in a home where the lamp was never turned on.

SEPT.
10
Sincerity is not synonymous with Christianity. Certainly, a Christian will be sincere, but it does not follow that because a man is sincere in what he believes he is a Christian.

Many people in Bible days were very sincere but very wrong. The prophets of Baal were so sincere that they tried all day to call down fire from heaven upon their sacrifice. They failed utterly, not for lack of sincerity, but because they were calling upon the wrong name.

Nicodemus was so sincere that he went to the trouble of finding Jesus during the night. Jesus told him that he was wrong and that without the new birth he could never even see the Kingdom of God.

The rich young ruler was so sincere that he ran and knelt before the Lord. He did not want for sincerity but Jesus told him that he did lack a personal committal of all that he had and was to the Son of God.

The Bible says, "For by grace are ye saved through faith; and that not of yourselves: it is the gift of God" (Ephesians 2:8).

SEPT. 11 Perhaps the most foolish aspect of sin is that it involves breaking a commandment that was given for the good and the protection of man.

The red light flashes at the railway crossing, not to impede our progress — but to warn us of danger. The man who ignores the signal is not only a criminal; he is a fool.

Sin is the wicked, wanton, useless rejection of that which is good and right in favor of that which is disgraceful and injurious.

This was the lament of Isaiah when he said, "For my people have committed two evils; they have forsaken me the fountain of living waters, and hewed them out cisterns, broken cisterns, that can hold no water" (Jeremiah 2:13).

The sinner leaves what is good in order to run after a disappointment.

SEPT. 12 There is a tendency to read the Bible in the third person—to make it apply to other people. This is natural because it puts us in an objective position and able to sit in judgment upon the rest of the world as if we were not part of it.

One of the greatest spiritual leaders of all time did much of his preaching in the first person. When he looked through the telescope of Old Testament prophecy and saw Calvary, he realized that it was his sin that nailed the Son of God to the cross. He did not point objectively at others and say, "He shed His blood for your sins." He included himself: "He was wounded for our transgressions, he was bruised for our iniquities: the chastisement of our peace was upon him and with his stripes we are healed" (Isaiah 53:5).

It is interesting to read the Bible in the third person but we will never know our own need until we read it in the first person. Put in your own name and read this verse as if you were the only person in the world and Christ had died for you.

SEPT.
13
Great ideas make great men. Small ideas make small men. Thoughts become things. Actions originate with ideas. That is why the Bible urges us to think righteously. "Set your affection on things above, not on things on the earth" (Colossians 3:2).

We may test our Christianity by our thoughts. Holy men think holy thoughts; profane men think profane thoughts. Clean men think clean and dirty men think dirty. The brutal think of brutality and the compassionate think of kindness. Righteousness dominates the mind of the Christian and sin controls the mind of the unsaved.

The Bible says that as man "thinketh in his heart, so is he" (Proverbs 23:7). Test the calibre of your thoughts and you probe the depth of your Christian experience.

SEPT.
14
There is a great wealth of prophetic material throughout the Bible and much of it has already been fulfilled. This is one reason we know that the Bible is the inspired Word of God.

It is possible, however, to become so intrigued by the study of the prophetic passages that we miss the personal message of the Bible to our own hearts and lives. In the Gospel of Matthew Jesus is described as separating the nations: "Before him shall be gathered all nations: and he shall separate them one from another, as a shepherd divideth his sheep from the goats" (Matthew 25:32).

This is prophetic and it is interesting to study and analyze the significance of this picture of the last days. It is also possible to become so utterly engrossed in this aspect of these verses that we do not apply them to ourselves by asking the question: In that day which group will I be with? Will I be on the right side or the wrong side?

Our relationship to Jesus Christ determines the side upon which we stand.

SEPT. 15   The greatest cause of broken homes is weddings to which the Son of God may not be invited.

When two unsaved people get married, Jesus is not a guest despite the fact that the ceremony may be performed in a Christian church, because the couple do not know Him.

If one member of the union is a Christian and the other is not, Jesus may not be present because they are entering into a relationship which is in direct disobedience to the command of the Bible: "Be ye not therefore partakers with them" (Ephesians 5:7).

When Jesus attended the wedding in Cana of Galilee, He changed it from a failure into a success. "And both Jesus was called, and his disciples to the marriage" (John 2:2).

Marriage may be difficult under any circumstances because it involves the union of two individual personalities, but it becomes a gigantic problem when Jesus Christ is left out.

SEPT. 16   Two human elements are used by the Holy Spirit to bring men to God. The first is gospel preaching and the second is gospel living.

The Apostle Paul told the church in Rome that the Word must be preached if people are to believe and be saved. "How shall they believe in him of whom they have not heard? and how shall they hear without a preacher?" (Romans 10:14).

The Apostle Peter declared that the unsaved might not respond to the preaching of the Gospel if they did not see it lived out in the lives of the Christians with whom they came into contact. He begs the children of God to live in such a manner that "they may by your good works, which they shall behold, glorify God in the day of visitation" (I Peter 2:12).

What a tragedy it would be to live in a land where the Gospel is preached and in a home where the Gospel is lived and refuse to accept Christ!

SEPT.
17   Probably half of the world's population have never had an adequate opportunity of hearing and accepting the message of the Gospel. This is true despite the fact that nearly two thousand years ago Jesus said, "And ye shall be witnesses unto me both in Jerusalem, and in all Judea, and in Samaria, and unto the uttermost part of the earth" (Acts 1:8).

This is indeed a sad commentary on the missionary efforts of the Christian church. Much more tragic is the fact that multitudes who have access to the message of Christ every-day have not yet accepted Him as Saviour.

Jesus said, "He that heareth my word, and believeth on him that sent me, hath everlasting life" (John 5:24). Millions have never heard, but you have. What a calamity to have heard and not to have accepted!

SEPT.
18   There were two men in the Bible who claimed to have kept the whole Jewish law. One was the rich young ruler. In response to Jesus' question about the law he said, "Master, all these have I observed from my youth" (Mark 10:20). The other was the Apostle Paul. He told the Christians at Philippi that as far as the law was concerned he was perfect, "Touching the righteousness which is in the law, blameless" (Philippians 3:6).

In both cases they were not ready for heaven despite the good law-abiding religious lives they had lived. Jesus told the rich young ruler that he did not have eternal life because he lacked one thing.

The Apostle Paul confessed that his faith in Jesus Christ did something for him spiritually that his good life had not been able to do. "For what the law could not do, in that it was weak through the flesh, God sending his own Son condemned sin in the flesh" (Romans 8:3).

It is a good thing to be a religious person, but to be right with God you must have Christ in your life.

SEPT. 19 The four gospels tell the story of Jesus, but each has a different emphasis. Matthew has written to show Jewish people that Jesus was the Messiah. Mark presents Jesus to the Gentiles as the servant of Jehovah. Luke gives an orderly account of the life of Jesus as seen by eyewitnesses. John inspires faith in Jesus as the Son of God.

Jesus urged the people of His day to read the Old Testament Scriptures because they told His story and today with the completed Bible, His command is even more important: "Search the scriptures; for in them ye think ye have eternal life: and they are they which testify of me" (John 5:39).

You can search for grains of truth in other books but if you want eternal life it is to be found in Christ and His story is found in the Bible.

SEPT. 20 It is possible for a man to sign his name at the bottom of the right creed and at the same time be far from God. King Saul was careful to observe all the written rules and make the proper sacrifices but Samuel condemned him, "Behold, to obey is better than sacrifice, and to hearken than the fat of rams" (I Samuel 15:22). Judah claimed to be God's representative nation, but the prophet Hosea declares the Word of God against the people, "For I desired mercy, and not sacrifice; and the knowledge of God more than burnt offerings" (Hosea 6:6).

Micah expressed the same principle to Israel, "What doth the Lord require of thee, but to do justly, and to love mercy, and to walk humbly with thy God?" (Micah 6:8).

The Pharisees during Jesus' life were orthodoxy personified, but Jesus rebuked them scathingly. "Ye make clean the outside of the cup and of the platter, but within they are full of extortion and excess" (Matthew 23:25).

Orthodoxy without the new birth is like a cup that is clean on the outside and filthy on the inside.

SEPT. 21 It pays to be a sinner. There is no doubt about it. Often the sharp operator may do well in politics, the man who cuts the corners may accumulate more money, and the undisciplined young person may have a greater number of good times.

But the Bible says there are other rewards for sin as well. The Bible says, "The soul of the transgressors shall eat violence; the lamp of the wicked shall be put out; the way of the transgressors is hard; evil pursueth sinners" (Proverbs 13:2, 9, 15, 21).

There is a constant undercurrent of misery and emptiness beneath the frivolity and wantonness of the sinner and there is destruction, hopelessness, and darkness at the end of his road.

SEPT. 22 The Christian church has always believed that Jesus is God. It is not enough that He is like God or even that He has some of the power of God. If He is to save us from our sin, He must actually be God.

This is apparent even to the man who reads the Bible casually. The attributes of God and Jesus are used so interchangeably that it is obviously describing the same deity in two different forms or personalities.

When John the Baptist announced the coming of Jesus to the Jordan River, he admitted in one sentence that Jesus was born after him but that he existed before him, "After me cometh a man which is preferred before me: for he was before me" (John 1:30).

Jesus confirms this conception by saying, "Before Abraham was, I am." Jesus is eternal. He has always been and always will be. This is an attribute of God and it makes no sense at all unless we realize that Jesus is God in the form of man.

When we trust Jesus Christ to save our souls, we are not depending upon the teachings of a great man; we are relying upon the power of God.

SEPT.
23

Before a man becomes a child of God he should understand that the Christian life involves a continual battle with the flesh. Before he has accepted Christ as his Saviour, he may cater to the desires of the flesh without restraint. There is no adequate reason to do otherwise.

In the life of a Christian, however, the spirit of man led by the Holy Spirit sits on the throne and the flesh must be subservient. This results in a struggle. "For the flesh lusteth against the Spirit; and the Spirit against the flesh, and these are contrary the one to the other" (Galatians 5:17).

At the end of the struggle there is the resurrection of the body and the change that makes us like Christ. Then the struggle of the flesh will be over forever and the Holy Spirit "shall change our vile body, that it may be fashioned like unto his glorious body" (Philippians 3:21).

SEPT.
24

Most people like to belong to something. That is why we join clubs and lodges and churches. In any organization we expect to be asked to fulfill certain requirements before our names may be written on the official roll.

The Bible talks about a Book that records the names of those who will be in heaven. It is called the Lamb's Book of Life. Some of the requirements for entrance are listed negatively in the book of Revelation: "And there shall in no wise enter into it anything that defileth, neither whatsoever worketh abomination, or maketh a lie: but they which are written in the Lamb's book of life" (Revelation 21:27).

It is nice for one's temporal influence to be a member of the right club, but it is necessary for his eternal welfare to be a member of the family of God. The membership books of the world will decay and be lost but the Book of Life will last forever. It is of the utmost importance that we become life-members.

SEPT.
25
Many times the Bible portrays God as knowing and seeing everything. The Old Testament says, "For the eyes of the Lord run to and fro throughout the whole earth, to shew himself strong in the behalf of them whose heart is perfect toward him . . . . Thine eyes are open upon all the ways of the sons of men" (II Chronicles 16:9; Jeremiah 32:19).

The thing that convinced Nathanael that Jesus was the Son of God was the fact that Jesus knew all about him before He met him: "Before that Philip called thee, when thou wast under the fig tree, I saw thee" (John 1:48).

Obviously, Jesus saw Nathanael as God saw him; He knew what kind of a man he was.

There is no one who escapes the eyes of the Lord. He has seen everything we have ever done, every place we have ever gone, and every thought that has ever crossed our minds. The grace of the Gospel is that He has offered to forgive us for our sins and give us eternal life.

SEPT.
26
There is no doubt that the Jews who became disciples of Jesus did so because they recognized Him as the Jewish Messiah. Each of the four gospel writers takes time to point out the Old Testament prophecies that were fulfilled in detail in Jesus.

When Andrew went back to bring Simon Peter to Jesus he said, "We have found the Messias, which is, being interpreted, the Christ" (John 1:41).

The promises of the Old Testament Scriptures have been expanded in their application by the Gospel which has made salvation possible not only to the Jew but also to all the Gentile peoples of the world. The Bible says, "That the Gentiles should be fellow heirs, and of the same body, and partakers in Christ by the gospel" (Ephesians 3:6).

Accept Christ as your Saviour and you accept the Messiah and become heir to the promises of the entire Bible to the people of God.

SEPT.
27
When a Christian lives a dedicated life the people of the world will question him and the Apostle Peter urges us to be prepared, "Be ready always to give an answer to every man that asketh you a reason of the hope that is in you" (I Peter 3:15).

If we cannot give a testimony of our salvation we are treading on dangerous ground because someday God will ask every man to give an account and instead of being the merciful Saviour who urges us to repent, He will be the righteous Judge.

When Peter speaks of the worldly people who ridiculed the Christians in his day he reminded them of the time of reckoning and warned that everyone of them, "Shall give account to him that is ready to judge the quick and the dead" (I Peter 4:5).

Better to be questioned about our holiness than judged for our sin.

SEPT.
28
It is an easy thing to set the hands of a broken watch. The second it is done the watch is absolutely accurate, as right as any watch in the world. The next second, however, it is wrong again, because the works are still broken. Adjusting the hands of a broken time piece is useless until the mechanism on the inside has been fixed.

Many people go through life like a broken watch. Occasionally, they take stock and adjust some aspect of their lives. It may be the hands of morality or ethics or business or marital relations, but within a few hours or days they are wrong again, because the trouble is on the inside.

The first step in reformation is regeneration, when the Spirit of God changes and "fixes" the heart. If the heart is right the actions will be right.

The Bible says, "Keep thy heart with all diligence; for out of it are the issues of life" (Proverbs 4:23). Righteousness starts with a changed heart.

SEPT.
29

Sometimes an unusual opportunity to get right with God is depicted in the Bible as a harvest.

When Jesus saw the woman of Samaria returning from the village followed by all her neighbors He raised His eyes above the green shoots of corn that would not be ripe for several months and focused His attention upon the harvest of human souls that was approaching. "Say not ye, There are yet four months, and then cometh harvest? behold, I say unto you, Lift up your eyes, and look on the fields; for they are white already to harvest" (John 4:35).

A harvest may either be gathered or destroyed. It may be saved or lost. Jeremiah lamented over Israel because the people had lived through a time of spiritual opportunity and neglected to turn to God: "The harvest is past, the summer is ended, and we are not saved" (Jeremiah 8:20).

This is a day of spiritual opportunity, a time of harvest. What a tragedy, to live in the midst of it and miss it!

SEPT.
30

The judgment of God may be a blessing in disguise because it may drive a man to God.

The Bible says, "Happy is the man whom God correcteth: therefore, despise not thou the chastening of the Lord" (Job 5:17). This was the experience of Job. His affliction made him turn to God as never before, and in the midst of it he said, "Though he slay me, yet will I trust him" (Job 13:15).

Sometimes a man becomes bitter and resentful because of the judgment of God. There were times when this happened to Moses and Joshua, and Elijah and David, and others. Elijah one time gave up in despair and the Bible says, "He requested for himself that he might die; and said, it is enough; now, O Lord, take away my life" (I Kings 19:4).

When trouble comes do not turn away from God. Trust Christ as your Saviour and throw yourself on the mercy of God.

OCT. 1 Spiritual armor is not meant to protect the body but the soul. The Christian may lose a physical battle but if he is right with God, he never loses a spiritual battle. He may lose the war of flesh and blood but he need not lose the war of the spirit. He is sustained in the face of temporal defeat by his confidence in God and the assurance of eternal victory.

The Bible says, "For though we walk in the flesh, we do not war after the flesh: For the weapons of our warfare are not carnal, but mighty through God to the pulling down of strong holds" (II Corinthians 10:3-4).

The Christian is the only man in the world about whom we can really say: "Bloody but unbowed." He knows the dignity of physical defeat, the fulfillment of material failure, and the peace of mortal pain.

OCT. 2 Some of the most persistent critics of the Bible are pseudo-intellectuals who have a little knowledge of a great many things but no profound understanding of anything.

It was Alexander Pope who said: "A little learning is a dangerous thing." Francis Bacon applied the principle directly to religion: "A little philosophy inclineth man's mind to atheism, but depth in philosophy bringeth men's minds about to religion."

The Bible asks the question: "Where is the wise? where is the scribe? where is the disputer of this world? hath not God made foolish the wisdom of this world?" (I Corinthians 1:20).

Then the answer is given: "But we preach Christ crucified . . . who of God is made unto us wisdom, and righteousness, and sanctification, and redemption" (I Corinthians 1:23, 30).

The wise man is not the one who knows a little about many things, but rather, the man who knows enough to accept Jesus Christ as his Saviour and thus come into personal contact with the Truth.

**OCT.
3**

The Bible teaches that there are two families in this world — the family of God and the family of the devil. "In this the children of God are manifest, and the children of the devil: whosoever doeth not righteousness is not of God" (I John 3:10).

This is why the worldly man cannot understand the godly man. They belong to different families. Their outlooks on life are different; often what one hates the other loves. They are headed in different directions; one is on the narrow way looking forward to everlasting life and the other is on the broad way with destruction looming ahead.

We belong to the family of God and have the life of God in us by virtue of our relationship to God's Son. The Bible says, "Whosoever shall confess that Jesus is the Son of God, God dwelleth in him, and he in God" (I John 4:15).

**OCT.
4**

The age of authority has given place to the scientific method. For generations the majority of people accepted the word of certain great men, or classic volumes, or ancient institutions as final. People did not ask questions. They accepted authority.

The Renaissance worked a *coup detat* upon the authorities and put the scientific method in office. Perhaps the rule of science and the material progress of civilization has been good. Certainly, it has opened new vistas on the horizons of human existence.

Born, bred, and educated in the groove of science, the modern man thinks he must analyze and prove everything, but when he comes to his religion he cannot adequately do so. He raises his infantile, scientific hands toward heaven and finds himself toying ignorantly with the shoelaces of the Almighty.

God has never been reached by science and never will be reached, because "God is a Spirit: and they that worship him must worship him in spirit and in truth" (John 4:24).

OCT.
5
Man says that the way to the top is up. The Bible says the way up is down. "He that humbleth himself shall be exalted" (Luke 14:11).

Man believes that the way to receive is to take. God says the way to receive is to give: "Give, and it shall be given unto you" (Luke 6:38).

Man thinks that the only way to live is to struggle for life. Jesus taught that the only way to find life is to lose it, "He that findeth his life shall lose it: and he that loseth his life for my sake shall find it" (Matthew 10:39).

The natural man cannot understand these things. The mind of man must be converted and the warp that sin has put into his intellect must be removed by the power of God before he can understand and accept the Word of God. The Psalmist prayed, "Open thou mine eyes, that I may behold wondrous things out of thy law" (Psalm 119:18).

OCT.
6
When a man becomes a Christian he takes his stand against the world and he is in direct line for the onslaught of the world.

In the early days of the church the unbelievers were constantly maligning the Christians. In Thessalonica they were accused of turning "the world upside down" (Acts 17:6-7; 19:37), and doing contrary to the decrees of Caesar and in Ephesus they were called robbers of churches and blasphemers.

These were lies, of course, but it took courage in those days for a person to take his stand for Christ in face of the opposition of a hostile world. Jesus warned His followers that this would happen, "Blessed are ye when men shall revile you, and persecute you, and shall say all manner of evil against you falsely, for my sake" (Matthew 5:11).

This is the challenge, and it takes strong men and courageous women to respond to it knowing the battle that is ahead.

OCT. 7

Even a casual glance through the Bible will prove that the fundamental principle of Christianity is faith. Faith is the rock upon which Christianity stands.

The Bible says, "For in Jesus Christ neither circumcision availeth any thing, nor uncircumcision; but faith which worketh by love. In all these things we are more than conquerors through him that loved us" (Galatians 5:6; Romans 8:37).

Science and intellect are vitally important to us as we grapple with the concrete problems of a material world, and they are helpful to our understanding of the Word of God. But spiritual victory over the world is not gained through intellectual proofs, or reasoning powers, or the scientific method. Victory over the world is accomplished through faith.

OCT. 8

It is not necessary to bow before an image that stands in a pagan temple to become an idolater. Thousands of people have become guilty of breaking the first commandment by allowing something in their lives to prevent them from accepting Jesus Christ as their Saviour.

A man's god may be his business, his pleasure, his sweetheart, his education, his habit, or many other things that are not considered idols. However, if anything separates a person from God, that thing is just as potent an idol in his life as the brass and stone and wooden images of the heathen.

The Bible says, "Behold, the Lord's hand is not shortened, that it cannot save; neither his ear heavy, that it cannot hear: But your iniquities have separated between you and your God" (Isaiah 59:1-2).

The power of God can save anyone, but God will not arbitrarily remove the idol in a man's life. This he must do himself.

OCT.
9
There is no particular virtue in acting foolishly or differently to prove that we are Christians. It is only when righteousness is involved that the Christian maintains the standard by being different from the world. If there is no real issue at stake, it is easy to become foolish in the eyes of the world to no purpose.

However, when we are born again, there is such a transformation that it is not long before we are at extreme poles from the people of the world. We may dress the same, eat the same, and work the same, but we are basically different and the unbelievers around us become aware of the difference.

The Apostle Peter says, "They think it strange that ye run not with them to the same excess of rioting, speaking evil of you" (I Peter 4:4).

The new are always a puzzle to the old. The corrupt man cannot understand the Christian. Bad men wonder at good men's conduct.

OCT.
10
It is a Bible principle that holiness brings suffering. It is possible to suffer without being holy, but it is not possible to be holy without suffering.

This world is not geared for the holy man. It is geared for the profane. Jesus proved this in His thirty-three short years of life in a world that could not stand holiness. Persecution and suffering were His constant companions and crucifixion was His human reward.

Jesus said, "The servant is not greater than his Lord. . . . In the world ye shall have tribulation" (John 13:16; 16:33). Peter was referring to these and other words of our Lord when he said, "Think it not strange concerning the fiery trial which is to try you, as though some strange thing happened unto you" (I Peter 4:12).

To become a Christian involves the gigantic challenge of serving God in a world that serves Satan, living a holy life in a world where holiness suffers, and going up in a world that is headed down.

OCT. 11 It is a dangerous thing to have the appearance of a Christian if you are not really a Christian.

It is like an army that has a strong front line but is unprotected in the rear. Such an army depends upon its frontal strength, only to fall someday before the enemy who attacks from behind.

To go to church without being a part of the living church, to sing about Christ without knowing Him personally, to read the Bible with the people of God without being born into the family of God is a dangerous condition.

The Bible describes such people as "Having a form of godliness, but denying the power thereof" (II Timothy 3:5).

We need to make sure that our faith is more than a profession, our Christianity more than a name, our testimony more than a speech, and our godliness more than a form.

OCT. 12 All sickness is not the direct result of sin in the life of the sick person. Jesus made this clear in the ninth chapter of John when the disciples asked Him about the blind man. Was his blindness the result of his own sin or that of his parents? Jesus answered, "Neither hath this man sinned, nor his parents: but that the works of God should be made manifest in him" (John 9:3).

However, the Apostle Paul declared that some sickness was the result of sin and that sometimes sin also resulted in the death of a Christian. When he urged the Corinthians not to partake of the Lord's Supper unless they were right with God he warned them, "For this cause many are weak and sickly among you, and many sleep" (I Corinthians 11:30).

Apparently, God will chastise His own child with disease and if he continues in disobedience God will remove him from the scene of action through death.

This is what John was talking about when he said, "There is a sin unto death" (I John 5:16). This is not loss of salvation, but the judgment of God upon a Christian for persistent disobedience.

OCT. 13 Salvation involves a great many changes in a man's life. One of the basic differences between the saved and the unsaved is the will. The unbeliever walks in accordance with the dictates of his own will. He says what he wants, goes where he chooses, and thinks as he pleases. In short, he lives his own life.

The Believer is guided by the will of God. His words, his pathway, and his thoughts are determined by the purposes of God for his life. He does not live his own life. He becomes a human tabernacle in which God lives. His own will is dissolved in the will of God.

The Bible says, "That he should no longer live the rest of his time in the flesh to the lusts of men, but to the will of God. For the time past of our life may suffice us to have wrought the will of the Gentiles" (I Peter 4:2-3).

OCT. 14 Nowhere in the Bible do we find the expression, "unpardonable sin." In the twelfth chapter of Matthew, Jesus speaks of the sin against the Holy Ghost and outlines two ages in which it cannot be forgiven — the age of law and the age of grace. The Apostle Paul makes it clear in the first chapter of Romans that even this sin will be forgiven during the Age of the Millenium.

The sin against the Holy Ghost is a national transgression. Israel commited it during the early days of the Age of Grace by rejecting the preaching of the Kingdom through the power of the Holy Ghost, thus blaspheming the Third Person of the Trinity. Not until the Millenium will the nation Israel have an opportunity to repent and accept the Kingdom.

In the meantime, there is no unpardonable sin except the obvious sin of permanently rejecting the mercy of God in Christ.

The Bible says, "To him give all the prophets witness, that through his name whosoever believeth in him shall receive remission of sins" (Acts 10:43).

OCT. 15 The person who commits suicide has capitulated before the onslaught of a very difficult world. Regardless of the method he may use he is removing himself from the scene of conflict because he just cannot stand the pressure any longer.

When we accept Jesus Christ as our Saviour we are born into the Family of God and our lives take on a spiritual stability that enables us to resist the temptation to escape from the problems of life. A suicide may be a strong character, a moral man, and a logical thinker, but at the point when he actually murders himself he has allowed himself to become an escapist, a coward, and a weakling.

Faith in God will give the Christian the power to stand when the average man would disintegrate. "Wherefore take unto you the whole armour of God, that ye may be able to withstand in the evil day, and having done all to stand" (Ephesians 6:13).

OCT. 16 If the Christian faith were to be robbed of the Deity of Christ, it would become no more than another philosophy of life—a good one perhaps, and certainly an ethical one — but just a system of philosophy. It is not what Jesus said that gives Christianity its unique position among other religions; it is who He is.

Two people may say exactly the same thing, but from the lips of one man it is a trivial statement while from the lips of another it makes history. Other religious leaders have urged their followers to live good lives but because they themselves were mere men they were not able to impart the power that a good life requires. Jesus Christ asks us to do things that humanly and naturally are impossible, but because He is God, He can give us the power to do them.

"In the beginning was the Word, and the Word was with God, and the Word was God. . . . And the Word was made flesh, and dwelt among us" (John 1:1, 14).

OCT. 17   Sin may be described as rebellion against God. This would be a tragic state at best but it is infinitely worse when we realize that we owe everything that is good about this world to God.

We have a roof over our heads in a world where thousands have no homes. We have clothes to wear in a world where multitudes sit in rags. We have food to eat while others grovel in the garbage heaps in an attempt to keep body and soul together.

All of this we owe to the grace of the living God. When we sin we rebel and disobey the commandments of the Divine Benefactor. Isaiah saw the same thing among his people in Old Testament days: "The ox knoweth his owner and the ass his master's crib: but Israel doth not know, my people doth not consider" (Isaiah 1:3).

The man who continues in his sin shows less gratitude than the dumb animal who refuses to bite the hand that feeds him.

OCT. 18   We might fight our own battles in this world if our only opposition came from material sources. We can resist flesh and blood and bone with our fists and muscles. We can oppose brains with brains, machines with machines, and words with words.

Even these physical and material foes create gigantic problems and tax the very best of our resources. Sometimes we come out of the battle the loser.

However, the Bible declares that in addition to these natural enemies we face a great spiritual world of unseen foes — foes that our fists cannot smash, our machines cannot crush and our brains cannot out-maneuver.

"For we wrestle not against flesh and blood, but against principalities, against powers, against the rulers of the darkness of this world, against spiritual wickedness" (Ephesians 6:11, 12).

Man, alone in the world, might get by without God, but man confronted by Satan and his hosts must have God.

OCT. 19

Sometimes we think of the human race as a group of people walking through life toward Eternity on a highway.

This is true to the Bible, but we should realize that everyone is not on the same road or headed in the same direction. There are two roads leading to two different destinations. Jesus said, "For wide is the gate and broad is the way that leadeth to destruction, and many there be which go in thereat: Because straight is the gate, and narrow is the way, which leadeth unto life, and few there be that find it" (Matthew 7:13-14).

All of us are on the broad way or the narrow way — headed for destruction or life. Christ makes the difference.

OCT. 20

People who die in their sins are described in the Bible as hopeless. When the Apostle Paul referred to the former condition of the Ephesians without Christ he calls them, "Strangers from the covenants of promise, having no hope, and without God in the world" (Ephesians 2:12).

The same Apostle comforts the Thessalonians in their bereavement by reminding them that in Christ they have hope, whereas outside of Christ there is no hope: "I would not have you to be ignorant, brethren, concerning them which are asleep, that ye sorrow not, even as others which have no hope" (I Thessalonians 4:13).

One of the most graphic words with which the Bible warns about hell is "darkness." Jesus uses the word to point out the hopelessness of the lost in hell. "Bind him hand and foot, and take him away, and cast him into outer darkness" (Matthew 22:13).

There is always hope in this life — hope of recovery, hope of a comeback, hope of a cure. In hell there is darkness — no hope.

OCT. 21 The civilized world has always recognized and condemned the sins of adultery and idolatry but few people ever think of wrath and envy as sins against God.

The Bible includes all of these in the same list, "Now the works of the flesh are manifest, which are these; adultery, fornication, uncleanness, wrath, strife, seditions, heresies, lasciviousness, idolatry, witchcraft, hatred, variance, emulations, envyings. They which do such things shall not inherit the kingdom of God" (Galatians 5:19-21).

This would make it impossible for any of us to be saved if God had not provided a way of escape, "But if we walk in the light, as he is in the light, we have fellowship one with another, and the blood of Jesus Christ his Son cleanseth us from all sin" (I John 1:7).

OCT. 22 People today are longing for security. Every peace conference and every United Nations meeting is a desperate effort on the part of the nations to bring security to this old world. In our own generation we have seen many things upon which we based our security collapse before our eyes and man is searching for something to hang on to in a world where everything seems so uncertain.

This world is doomed. There is no security to be had from it, but in Jesus Christ we can find the thing we crave. The Bible says, "And thou shalt be secure, because there is hope; yea, thou shalt take thy rest in safety" (Job 11:18).

This passage is in the Old Testament but Jesus confirmed the same principle when He said, "Go ye therefore . . . and, lo, I am with you alway, even unto the end of the world" (Matthew 28:19, 20).

After this world has ended, if our faith is in Christ, we will have security not only for time but for eternity.

OCT. 23

The Bible does not frown upon pleasure because there is no evil in pleasure as such. The tendency of the world is to become so completely absorbed in pleasure that God and the church fade into the background and take a secondary position.

When this happens any sort of pleasure, though it may be absolutely innocent, is wrong. It is not wrong to eat a big meal; it is wrong to let that meal keep us away from church on Sunday night. It is not wrong to play golf; it is wrong to let golf take the place of our private devotions. It is not wrong to join a club; it is wrong if the club takes precedence over the activity of the church.

The Bible says, "This know also, that in the last days . . . men shall be lovers of pleasure more than lovers of God" (II Timothy 3:1, 4).

OCT. 24

The disciples thought the rich young ruler could never be saved because his wealth had separated him so far from God. Sometimes we look upon certain people as hopeless cases and often a man thinks of himself as a lost cause spiritually.

These people fall into two classes: those who have sinned so deeply that we conclude the way back is just too far and they will never make it, or those who have resisted the gospel invitation so long that they have become unchangeably set in their ways.

The Bible does not consider anyone as a hopeless case. It does not matter how much a man has sinned, how far away he has wandered, or how often he has rejected Christ, he is still included in the "whosoever" of salvation.

When the disciples looked with despair at the retreating form of the rich young ruler, Jesus said, "With men it is impossible, but not with God: for with God all things are possible" (Mark 10:27).

There is no impossible case with God.

OCT. 25 A good friend is one who stays with you when everyone else is against you. This kind is very rare. The Bible says that even a person's mother and father will forsake him under certain conditions. "When my father and mother forsake me, then the Lord will take me up" (Psalm 27:10).

If we do not know Jesus Christ as our Saviour, we will have no one to whom we can turn when everyone else is gone from us. What a tragedy to be without friends! What an infinitely greater tragedy to be without God.

Jesus must have known how unreliable people could be when He promised, "I will never leave thee, nor forsake thee" (Hebrews 13:5).

Friends may shun us. Even our mothers and fathers may turn their backs upon us, but Christ will accept us with open arms the moment we turn to Him.

OCT. 26 During a terrific storm the Apostle Paul restored faith among a crew that had completely despaired of ever seeing land again. On that occasion he said, "Be of good cheer, for I believe God" (Acts 27:22).

This is the only final remedy for fear — faith in God. Fear of life is foreign to the man who believes God. Fear of sickness becomes impotent in the man who believes God. Fear of trouble is absent from the man who believes God. Fear of war is a stranger to the man who believes God. Fear of death is not a part of the man who believes God.

Christianity does not involve a passive faith that is not concerned about all of these important things, but it does demand an active faith in Jesus Christ that destroys the paralyzing fear that man has of all of these. There is a great difference between confident concern and paralyzing fear. Everyone is anxious about world affairs and personal problems, but the Christian is confident of the outcome.

OCT. 27 Man in the natural state is described in the Bible as dead spiritually. Death is a condition without hope. This hopelessness of sinful man is often compared to darkness — darkness, because man cannot see beyond the grave. He is in the dark and that darkness is an eternal hopelessness.

The advent of the Son of God gave sinners the potential of everlasting life through personal contact with Jesus Christ. That is one of the reasons that He is called the Life and the Light.

The Bible says, "In him was life; and the life was the light of men. And the light shineth in darkness" (John 1:4, 5).

The hopelessness is removed from a man's heart and the darkness is dispelled from his mind when he is united by faith to Christ and shares in His life.

OCT. 28 The love and joy and peace and all the other blessings that the child of God receives when he trusts Christ as his Saviour are very real and absolutely priceless.

However, Jesus warned the people of His day that in addition to the blessings there would be burdens. The joy of the Lord would be accompanied by the jeering of the world and the peace of God would be realized in the midst of persecution.

This is what He was talking about when He said, "Which of you, intending to build a tower, sitteth not down first, and counteth the cost . . . lest haply, after he hath laid the foundation, and is not able to finish it, all that behold it begin to mock him, Saying, This man began to build, and was not able to finish" (Luke 14:28-30).

This is why many have fallen by the wayside of a feeble attempt to act like a Christian. It is necessary to count the cost first, and then reach up by faith and lay hold on the resources of heaven that can give us the strength to go through.

OCT.
29
The rich farmer was a fool because he neglected eternity. Out of the forever that was ahead of him he segregated a few short years of time and laid away a store of goods not for eternity — but "for many years."

He had forgotten that "The days of our years are three-score years and ten; and if by reason of strength they be four-score years, yet is their strength labour and sorrow, for it is soon cut off, and we fly away" (Psalm 90:10).

He planned for this world and he lost for this world and the next. He was ready for this life but he was not ready for the life to come. He had prepared for time but had failed to prepare for eternity.

Jesus told the story and then added, "So is he that layeth up treasures for himself, and is not rich toward God" (Luke 12:21).

OCT.
30
Any book is enhanced to some extent if we know the author personally. If we love the author, the book becomes even more valuable. However, it is by no means necessary to know or love the author of most books before we can enjoy them. Thousands of volumes are read every day by people who will never come into contact with the writers.

The Bible is the only book that necessitates a personal relationship with the Author before we can appreciate it. It is essential to know God and have the resulting illumination of the Holy Spirit before the Bible will mean to us what it should. One good test of Christianity is our love of the Book. We may never understand it all, but when we know God it speaks to us as the voice of God. That is why the Psalmist said, "Open thou mine eyes, that I may behold wondrous things out of thy law" (Psalm 119:18).

OCT. 31 Frequently the voice of God is heard through other people.

The greatest of Israel's Kings was called to the throne through the medium of another man. God spoke to Samuel and Samuel spoke to David, "And the Lord said, Arise, anoint him: for this is he."

God always has His prophets and His preachers and His messengers. They may be a mother, a father, an intimate friend, or a Sunday school teacher. The pulpits of the uttermost parts of the earth and the Jerusalems of our modern world are filled by godly people who heard the voice of God in many cases through the medium of another person.

This is one of the Divine methods of leadership, but there are many who have never heard God speak through other people. For these and for all of us God has put His words in print so that we can hear from heaven whenever we open the Bible.

Here is the voice of God for the person who is burdened with the unbearable weight of his sin: "This is my blood of the new testament, which is shed for many for the remission of sins" (Matthew 26:28).

NOV.
1
There are two words for God in the Old Testament. *Elohim* is an impersonal expression that may be used of heathen deities as well as the true God. *Jehovah* is the personal name of God given for the first time to Moses at the burning bush.

Elohim is the God of the whole world, sinners and saints alike. Jehovah is the God of the redeemed. Elohim is a title and Jehovah is a personal name.

When David said, "The Lord is my shepherd; I shall not want" (Psalm 23:1), he used the sacred name Jehovah with all of its implication of redemption. Then he connected himself with God by using the personal pronoun.

It is one thing to say that God saves men from sin. It is quite another thing to say, "God saves me from sin." This is what David implied toward the end of his life when he lifted his face toward heaven and said, "Jehovah, my shepherd."

NOV.
2
The Bible says, "As newborn babes, desire the sincere milk of the word, that ye may grow thereby" (I Peter 2:2).

A young Christian is a spiritual baby, and a baby necessitates birth.

A baby may be born in a church, in a home, on the street, at work, or anywhere else, but it is not a baby until it is born.

A baby may be born with inadequate help or with the best and most experienced in the world, but it must be born.

It is not necessarily important that a man know when he was born into the family of God or how or where, but it is pre-eminently important that he know he has experienced the new birth.

The Bible says, "Of his own will begat he us with the word of truth, that we should be a kind of first fruits of his creatures" (James 1:18).

NOV. 3   It is extremely easy to be the same as other people, but it takes a real man to be different. It takes no effort to go with the crowd. That is the popular thing to do, but it takes character to go God's way. In any language the simplest word that you can say is "yes." There are thousands of "yes-men," but God is looking for people who know how to say "no."

Some of the celebrities of Jesus' day really believed what He said, but they were afraid of the crowd. They did not want to lose the applause of the people, and they refused to stand with Christ. The Bible describes them as men who "loved the praise of men more than the praise of God" (John 12:43).

The Apostle Peter had learned the secret of standing alone for God in opposition to men if necessary. He spoke for them all when he said, "We ought to obey God rather than men" (Acts 5:29).

NOV. 4   The resurrection is part of the Christian faith. Without it Christianity means nothing. The laws of the Bible have become the basis of the code of laws of most of the civilized nations of the world. The ethics of Jesus have affected the society even of those who do not claim to be Christian. His example has been the ideal of good men for two thousand years, and His religion has put steeples into the skylines of every modern city.

All of these things stand without meaning as monuments that are a mockery to civilized man unless the resurrection of Jesus Christ from the grave is a reality upon which we can depend.

The Apostle Paul says, "If Christ be not raised, your faith is vain; ye are yet in your sins" (I Corinthians 15:17). Christianity and eternal life through Christ is made possible only by the resurrection.

NOV.
5
Intense love on the human level is usually characterized by a desire to be near the person we love. How barren human love becomes when lovers are content to be apart.

Burning within the breast of the fervent Christian is a desire to be near his Lord and have fellowship with Him. This is the secret of answered prayer. Jesus said, "If ye abide in me, and my words abide in you, ye shall ask what ye will, and it shall be done unto you" (John 15:7).

NOV.
6
In many places the Bible describes the Christian as a person who is sober. "The end of all things is at hand: be ye therefore sober, and watch unto prayer" (I Peter 4:7).

Sobriety is the opposite of intoxication and intoxication can be defined as a state in which our powers of perception have been blurred.

Usually we think of alcohol as the only cause of intoxication, but there are many other things that can do the same thing. A man may be intoxicated with money, business, pleasure, education, or the appetites of his body. An undue emphasis on any of these things can cause an intoxication of the soul so great that we cannot see, hear, or understand. Our sense of spiritual perception has become blind, deaf, and dead.

This is what the prophet was talking about when he said, "We grope for the wall like the blind, and we grope as if we had no eyes: we stumble at noonday as in the night; we are in desolate places as dead men" (Isaiah 59:10).

When a man becomes a child of God, the eyes of his soul are opened, the ears of his soul are unstopped, and the heart of his soul is quickened.

NOV.
7
Christianity results in a regeneration. The Bible describes man as being alive physically but dead spiritually.

As a rock is dead to plant life and a plant is dead to animal life and an animal is dead to human life, so a human is dead to spiritual life. There is a vast eternal world to which the natural man is blind, deaf and dead.

When this kind of man commits his life to God through faith in Christ, he becomes alert to the spiritual world. The Bible says, "And you hath he quickened, who were dead in trespasses and sins" (Ephesians 2:1). Jesus said, "I am the life: no man cometh unto the Father, but by me" (John 14:6).

NOV.
8
From many standpoints man is insignificant. Most of us are forgotten shortly after we die. A few of the more important have their names in the history books. However, the average student of history has difficulty remembering who these were and what they did.

The rocks last a great deal longer than men in this world. Tourists may still walk on the same stones as the Apostle Paul walked. The stones are still there but Paul has been gone for nearly two milleniums.

No wonder Job asked the question, "What is man, that thou shouldest magnify him? and that thou shouldest set thine heart upon him?" (Job 7:17).

Obviously, man has some value that the rocks and the trees and the animals do not have. When God made man he was no different than these material animal things. But when God breathed into him the breath of life, he became a living soul — with the potential of sinning and being lost forever, or of accepting Christ and being saved forever.

NOV. 9
This is a chaotic world. Everyone knows it without being told by a preacher or a politician.

Only a few years ago we used to talk about countries that were "trouble spots." Today it is difficult to pin point locations on our map of the world that are not "trouble spots."

It is little wonder that our mental institutions are overflowing and hundreds of our people are experiencing nervous breakdowns.

Jesus undoubtedly knew that there would be a time when men's hearts would fail them for fear and they would need the stabilizing influence of personal contact with God through faith in Christ.

In days that were dark for the disciples, He brought hope into their lives with His promise of peace: "Peace I leave with you, my peace I give unto you: not as the world giveth, give I unto you. Let not your heart be troubled, neither let it be afraid" (John 14:27).

NOV. 10
The Apostle Paul told the Christians at Ephesus that the love of God "passeth knowledge." It is beyond the mental capacity and practical experience of man to understand. He has never seen such love and it is difficult for him to comprehend it.

We are familiar with the kind of love which embraces the good and the beautiful and the attractive. It is a source of wonder to us that the love of God also includes the evil, and the ugly, and the repulsive.

The Bible says, "But God commendeth his love toward us, in that, while we were yet sinners, Christ died for us" (Romans 5:8).

We do not have to reform ourselves until we have reached a point of goodness at which God can love us. God has made provision for us as we are — in our sin and dirt and debauchery.

NOV.
11
Sometimes the spiritual prodigal is one who has been in close fellowship with God.

In the New Testament Peter is represented as a man who was closer to the Lord than most of the other disciples. He was often the spokesman for the twelve. He was one of the three on the Mount of Transfiguration. He was the only one that tried to walk on the water, and it was he who first put the confession of Messiahship into words. But it was Peter's denial that is described as the flagrant case among the twelve.

Extreme contrasts in life often lie very close to one another. Perhaps this is why the Bible says, "Wherefore let him that thinketh he standeth take heed lest he fall" (I Corinthians 10:12).

What a consolation to the backslider to know that there is always a welcome to the one who comes to his senses and decides to come back to God.

NOV.
12
A chain is useless when one link is broken. An automobile is powerless when one wheel is off. The absence of one small part from a huge machine will often stop it completely, and when a man disobeys one part of the law, he has broken the law.

It is not necessary to commit every crime known to man in order to be a criminal. One crime makes a criminal. A man does not have to break all the laws of God before he is a sinner. When he disobeys God at one point he is just as guilty as if he broke every law God ever revealed.

"For whosoever shall keep the whole law, and yet offend in one point, he is guilty of all" (James 2:10). It does not require the judgment of a court and jury to prove that we have all broken God's law. The jury that sits in the seat of our own conscience has already brought in the verdict, "Guilty." That is why all men need a Saviour and the mercy of a Heavenly Father.

NOV.
13

Some people have never accepted Christ as their Saviour because they have lived in homes where religion has been foisted upon them constantly. Often this forced religion has not been supported by lives that exemplify the Spirit of Christ.

Sometimes the quiet testimony of a life lived for God has more effect than a great deal of potent preaching.

After Jesus had raised Lazarus from the grave, many people came to Bethany and when they had seen what Christ had done for Lazarus, they went away believing on Jesus.

The Bible says, "Because that by reason of him many of the Jews went away, and believed on Jesus" (John 12:11).

Although some have been the objects of a forced religion, there are others who have been exposed to effective Christian lives for years and have not yet accepted the Gospel.

NOV.
14

It is ordained in this world that people will die. Some leave this life prematurely, some live a normal span, and a few are blessed with extremely old age.

There are those who put in a miserable existence, others who live a passive life during which nothing very important happens, and a minority whose lives are filled with excitement and intensity.

Regardless of the number of years or the degree of activity, everyone must eventually die. The only people who can face death with confidence are those who know God. In the Old Testament, David said, "Yea, though I walk through the valley of the shadow of death, I will fear no evil: for thou art with me" (Psalm 23:4). In the New Testament Paul said, "For I am now ready to be offered, and the time of my departure is at hand" (II Timothy 4:6).

David had no fear of death because he knew God. Paul was ready to die because he was in touch with God through faith in Christ.

**NOV.
15** Jesus told His disciples about an ambitious farmer — a man who surveyed his work and then said, "I will pull down my barns, and build greater" (Luke 12:18).

At the end of the story God called the man a fool. He was not a fool because of his ambition. It is a good quality in any man's character to have a great objective in life and work toward achieving it.

This farmer was a fool because he had no place in his ambitious life for God. He had never realized that the first step of a good man's ambition is to be sure he is right with God. Ambition sat on the throne of his life and success clouded the sanctuary of his soul. The Bible says, "Thou shalt have no other Gods before me" (Exodus 20:3).

**NOV.
16** In the Old Testament, death is described as "the valley of the shadow." In the New Testament, it is compared to a departure.

The Apostle Paul thought about his own life and death and then said, "I am in a strait betwixt two, having a desire to depart, and to be with Christ; which is far better" (Philippians 1:23).

In the ancient language the word "depart" means to break up a temporary camp and move on to a permanent home.

For the man who has trusted Jesus Christ as his Saviour, this world is a temporary camp. He is here as an ambassador on business for the King of Kings. When he dies he goes home to the country of which he is a citizen.

The Bible says, "For we know that if our earthly house of this tabernacle were dissolved, we have a building of God, an house not made with hands, eternal in the heavens" (II Corinthians 5:1).

For the man who does not know the Lord, death is still the dreaded "valley of the shadow." For the Christian death means "promotion to glory."

NOV.
17
It is much easier to work alone than it is to cooperate with others. Disagreement is much more human than agreement. A child may produce discord from the keys of a piano. It takes a trained and disciplined musician to bring out harmony.

We will never find anyone who is identical to us. Everyone has a slightly different way of doing things and to some extent at least, a different form of believing.

It is the ideal of the Bible that in Christ people who have many divergencies of opinions and background and method should be able to cooperate around the major thrust of the Christian message — which is salvation through faith in Christ for a world that is lost in sin.

This was the longing of the Apostle when he wrote, "Fulfil ye my joy, that ye be likeminded, having the same love, being of one accord, of one mind" (Philippians 2:2).

NOV.
18
It is impossible for any man to be completely isolated from the rest of the world. At some period in our lives other people who live around us have an effect upon us. Most of the things we learn, we have copied from others. We model our lives after them.

The Apostle Paul realized this and urged people to watch him closely and then follow in his footsteps. To the Thessalonians he was able to say, "As ye know what manner of men we were among you . . . And ye became followers of us, and of the Lord" (I Thessalonians 1:5-6).

It is possible to live so sincerely for God that we with the Apostle Paul can rejoice when our family and friends walk in our footsteps. There are many men who would be horrified to see their sons patterning their lives after them because they know that they are not living for God. May God help us to be the kind of persons that others can follow without going wrong.

NOV. 19 The flag of the Christian faith is our love for one another.

It is important that we believe sound doctrine but it is possible to be thoroughly orthodox without demonstrating the love of God in our contact with others. The Pharisees were orthodox to the core, but Jesus said that they needed to repent of their sins.

It is essential that we live a Christian life. Christian conduct is the natural outcome of an experience with God. However, it is possible for an adherent of a heathen religion to have the same list of "do's" and "don'ts" as a Christian.

When a person is born into the family of God, he partakes of the life of God and the love of God and this love flowing out toward others is the banner of discipleship.

Jesus said, "By this shall all men know that ye are my disciples, if ye have love one to another" (John 13:25).

NOV. 20 It is relatively easy to ask questions that no one can answer. Two kinds of people are masters of this sort of interrogation — skeptics and children.

There are four kinds of questions: 1) Those that do not make sense; 2) those to which there are answers, but as yet man does not know them; 3) those to which there are answers that involve principles beyond the capacity of man; 4) those to which man does know the answers.

In the field of religion many people spend a great deal of time arguing about the first three and fail miserably to live in accordance with the answers we have.

We do not know when Christ will come back, but He assures us that He will come, "If I go and prepare a place for you, I will come again, and receive you unto myself" (John 14:3).

NOV. 21 The power of God can transform the vilest sinner into a saint and the same power can make a great saint out of an ordinary Christian.

The Apostle Paul testifies to the fact that he was a notorious sinner but that Christ saved him, "This is a faithful saying, and worthy of all acceptation, that Christ Jesus came into the world to save sinners; of whom I am chief" (I Timothy 1:15).

James assures us that one of the greatest of Old Testament prophets was an ordinary man with the same feelings and weaknesses, and longings as others, "Elias was a man subject to like passions as we are" (James 5:17).

We know the vast potential that was realized in the Apostle Paul. We are familiar with the prayer power of Elijah, but we have always thought of these as unusual men. Actually, the only unusual thing about Paul and Elijah is that they were completely surrendered to God.

NOV. 22 Anyone who wishes can accept Christ at any time, but it is clearly indicated in the Bible that at some times it is easier to do so than at others.

There are moments in our lives when we are so close to the Kingdom of God that it would be a simple matter to step in. There are other times when so much separates us from God that we feel as if our cry is too weak to reach Him.

Perhaps this is why Isaiah urged the people of his day, "Seek ye the Lord while he may be found, call ye upon him while he is near" (Isaiah 55:6).

Many people have lived through periods of spiritual opportunity without responding and have allowed themselves to be separated from God by months and sometimes years of sin and worldliness.

NOV. 23 Christianity carries with it no exemption from suffering. The promises of the Bible do not provide freedom from sorrow or sickness or difficulty or even physical death. Jesus Christ assured His followers of divine strength and companionship in the midst of these things.

As a matter of fact, the Christian assumes a greater potential for trials by his very faith because in addition to the normal burdens and problems of human life, he shares the opposition of a profane world to a holy God. As a Christian he is in direct line for the assault of the world, the flesh and the devil which are in constant warfare against righteousness.

The Bible says, "For unto you it is given in the behalf of Christ, not only to believe on him, but also to suffer for his sake" (Philippians 1:29).

NOV. 24 The Christian faith presupposes a love that is both vertical and horizontal — one that fixes its eyes through faith in Christ on heaven and wraps its arms in compassion around the misery of earth.

Humanitarianism that has no personal contact with God is not Christian and any professed love for God that is oblivious to the need of man is not Christian.

The first commandment looks toward heaven: "Thou shalt love the Lord thy God" (Deuteronomy 6:5). The second looks toward earth, "and thy neighbour as thyself" (Leviticus 19:18).

Jesus said, "Not everyone that saith unto me, Lord, Lord, shall enter into the kingdom of heaven; but he that doeth the will of my Father which is in heaven" (Matthew 7:21).

The Apostle James declared that "Faith without works is dead" (James 2:24).

A man may be a humanitarian without being a Christian but he cannot be a Christian without being a humanitarian.

NOV. 25 It is difficult for us to understand why God would condemn heathen people who have never heard the Gospel. The Bible does not give us the complete answer, but it does assure us that God will deal justly and wisely with all men.

We *do* know that people who have heard the Gospel will be lost eternally if they do not accept it and they will be without excuse. "How shall we escape, if we neglect so great salvation?" (Hebrews 2:3).

In the midst of pondering the eternal doom of the heathen — which is not our problem — it is possible to neglect the salvation of our own souls — which is our problem.

NOV. 26 The godly life of a Christian will be a continual source of irritation to the world. Nothing will convict a man of sin as pointedly as the Spirit-filled life of a saint.

The Apostle Paul told one group of Christians that their faith in God was a constant reminder to unbelievers that they were lost just as it is a token to believers that they are saved. "With one mind striving together for the faith of the gospel which is to them an evident token of perdition, but to you of salvation, and that of God" (Philippians 1:27, 28).

The man who is aggravated by holiness is obviously a sinner. If he were not, he would rejoice in holiness and it would be a source of encouragement to him.

A good test of our spiritual standing is our reaction to purity, honesty, truth, goodness, and everything that is a part of holiness. Do these things rub us the wrong way or are we in line with them?

**NOV.
27**   The Bible emphasizes the unlimited value of each individual. God is not concerned only about great masses of people. He has made provision for the world's multitudes but on a personal basis.

Jesus declared, "The very hairs of your head are all numbered" (Matthew 10:30). Then to point up the inestimable value of one man He asked, "For what shall it profit a man if he shall gain the whole world, and lose his own soul?" (Mark 8:36).

There is sufficient grace in the heart of God to wrap its arms around a whole world of people. There is enough potential in one individual for God to make this all-embracing grace available to each one of us as though we were the only person in the world.

**NOV.
28**   The Bible describes the Christian as a citizen of heaven, "For our conversation (citizenship) is in heaven; from whence also we look for the Saviour, the Lord Jesus Christ" (Philippians 3:20).

The Apostle Paul was proud of his Roman citizenship and used it occasionally to good advantage, but he was acutely conscious of his heavenly citizenship and his great desire was to make sure that he always acted as a citizen of heaven should act.

When he wrote to the Philippian Christians, he reminded them of their allegiance to Christ and the Gospel and then he said, "Only let your conversation (conduct) be as it becometh the Gospel of Christ" (Philippians 1:27).

It is a sad state of affairs when a Christian gives a poor impression to his fellow citizens by failing to act as a child of God should act.

NOV. 29 There are nearly three thousand languages in this modern world. Some of the Bible has been translated into one thousand of these, but the other two thousand have none.

If we had happened to speak any one of these two thousand languages, we never would have seen the Word of God in print, and we might not have known the way of salvation.

In this country, we have been surrounded by the printed page — in tracts, books, newspapers, magazines, and Bibles. What a tragedy it would be to be lost forever with clearly written instructions of the way out at our fingertips.

The Bible says, "These things have I written unto you . . . that you may know that ye have eternal life, and that ye may believe on the name of the Son of God" (I John 5:13).

NOV. 30 There are some complicated passages in the Bible. Some churches interpret them in one way and others think they mean something else.

However, there are a number of fundamental truths about which there can be no doubt. One of these is the fact that salvation may be had through faith in Jesus Christ and in no other way. Peter said, "There is none other name under heaven given among men, whereby we must be saved" (Acts 4:12).

Another is that the only atonement for sin is the shed blood. "Without shedding of blood is no remission" (Hebrews 9:22).

A third is that the miracle of the new birth must take place before a man can be a part of the Kingdom of God. "Except a man be born again, he cannot see the kingdom of God" (John 3:3).

When a man trusts Christ as his Saviour, his sins are cleansed in the blood of Christ, and he is born into the family of God. These things we know.

DEC. 1
Perhaps the most difficult thing for any man to do is to admit that he is wrong. It requires wisdom to see our mistakes and courage to admit them.

The Bible declares that all men are wrong. That is, wrong in their relationship to God. The Bible uses the word sin to describe this condition, "For all have sinned, and come short of the glory of God" (Romans 3:23).

Most people refuse to see themselves in this universal statement, but the Word of God includes all of us.

If we have never admitted our sin, we will never ask the question, "What must I do to be saved?" (Acts 16:30). When we are big enough to ask this question we will get God's answer. "The fear of man bringeth a snare: but whoso putteth his trust in the Lord shall be safe" (Proverbs 29:25).

DEC. 2
It is impossible to live without exercising faith. The Christian has faith in Jesus Christ. The self-styled rationalist puts his faith in the observations of his own senses of perception and the conclusions of his own mind.

There is an idea abroad that we must choose between rationalism and faith. Actually, in the Christian man there is no need for a choice between these two, but rather an intelligent combination. The Christian does not cease to think, but he does recognize the existence of a whole world of ideas and values to which faith is the only bridge.

There is nothing wrong with rationalism as long as it does not include atheism, but the senses and the mind are able to carry man no farther than the perimeter of the material world. As he crosses the threshold of the spiritual universe man needs to remember the words of the Bible: "Trust in the Lord with all thine heart; and lean not unto thine own understanding. . . . It is better to trust in the Lord than to put confidence in man" (Proverbs 3:5, Psalm 118:8).

DEC. 3

Methuselah lived 969 years. Apparently apart from the gigantic span of his life, this man did very little. He is not a source of inspiration nor is he a model of accomplishment. He is just a name that existed for a long time.

There are many others in the Bible who lived for much shorter periods, but we turn to them constantly for help. Perhaps the most condensed life of all was that of our Lord. He lived for only thirty-three years and His active ministry lasted only three, but in that time He accomplished a work that forever closed the gap between the sinfulness of man and the holiness of God. The Bible says, "See then that ye walk circumspectly, not as fools, but as wise; Redeeming the time, because the days are evil" (Ephesians 5:15-16).

The important thing is not how long we live, but what we accomplish for God *while* we live.

DEC. 4

There are only two sources from which we can learn what Jesus did and taught. One is the Christian Church. The other is the Christian Bible. If it were not for these two, our information about Christ would be so fragmentary, we could not build a religion on it.

Both of our sources tell us that certain basic ingredients are necessary if we are to be Christians — implicit faith in the Deity of Christ, recognition and confession of sin, the regenerating power of the Holy Spirit which entitles us to belong to the family of God, and a life that is controlled by the ethics of Jesus.

If any of these are missing, we may have some sort of religion, but we are not Christians.

"Search the Scriptures, for in them ye think ye have eternal life and they are they which testify of me" (John 5:39).

DEC. 5

The Bible says, "That which is born of the flesh is flesh" (John 3:6). Man would like to think that flesh can be changed — that it has been changed by the gradual process of evolution in the past and that science and education and training can change it in the present.

Of course, there is not one single piece of evidence to indicate that the flesh of man has ever at any time been any different from what it is today, and the Bible holds forth no promise of a change in the future.

If the need of man is to be met, an entirely new principle must be introduced — the spirit.

The flesh will always be flesh, but when a man trusts Christ as his Saviour he is regenerated — spiritual life is introduced, the life of God Himself, the life that can control the flesh.

DEC. 6

We can worship God in the woods with a shot gun over our arm, in a boat with a line dangling over the side in a car on the open road.

But we probably won't. Most people could count on the fingers of one hand the prayers that have passed through their minds in the woods, a boat, or a car.

It takes two hours or less to worship God the way Christ set the example — in the synagogues of His day, and the way the early Christians obviously did — in groups with others in a given place at a specific time.

This is what the modern church provides. Without it we rob ourselves of an essential part of a balanced personality.

The person who has accepted Christ as his Saviour will want to go to church. He will believe the Psalmist when he said, "Blessed are they that dwell in thy house: they will be still praising thee" (Psalm 84:4).

DEC.
7

When we accept Jesus Christ as our Saviour, we are born spiritually. We become the possessors of spiritual life.

This new life responds to the Holy Spirit and the communion between our new spirit and the Spirit of God gives us confidence in the fact that we have become the children of God.

Salvation is not merely a group of facts which we accept as the truth but it is the formation of a completely new creature who is in conscious communion with God.

The Apostle Paul was aware of this spiritual fellowship with God that gave him the assurance of his salvation.

"The Spirit itself beareth witness with our spirit, that we are the children of God" (Romans 8:16).

DEC.
8

Many people become Christians for what they think they may get out of it. A poor man sometimes accepts Christ because he thinks God may make him rich. Certain men will often turn to the Lord because they feel it may relieve them of some of the pressure of discrimination. A prisoner may make a religious decision because he thinks it will unlock the penitentiary doors. Often a person who is desperately ill will yield his life to God in order to be healed.

Occasionally, a man responds to the Divine invitation because he is sick of his sin and longs to be right with God regardless of the material consequences. He has something of the spirit of the three men who faced the fiery furnace in the book of Daniel. They hoped God would help them, but their faith did not depend upon personal profit. They said, "If it be so, our God whom we serve is able to deliver us from the burning fiery furnace, he will deliver us, but if not, be it known unto thee, O king, that we will not serve thy gods" (Daniel 3:17-18).

DEC.
9
It is natural to associate wealth with satisfaction. We think that if we were well-situated financially, if we had no need of material things, we would be satisfied.

What a tragic mistake! Some have achieved all of these things, but they are miserable — because money cannot buy the most important needs of man. The essential spiritual values are not to be purchased in the warehouses of the world.

Great wealth is no assurance of satisfaction. It is faith in Jesus Christ that unlocks the treasure houses of heaven and makes them available.

The blessings of God are free: "Ho, every one that thirsteth, come ye to the waters, and he that hath no money; come ye, buy, and eat; yea, come, buy wine and milk without money and without price" (Isaiah 55:1).

DEC.
10
The ability of any man to know right from wrong and to do right is determined by his love for God.

The person who loves God with his whole heart will spend time in fellowship with God. The more time that is spent in fellowship with God, the better a man will know God. As he learns to know God better, he begins to see the world as God sees it and is given by God the ability to judge accurately between right and wrong.

When the Apostle Paul prayed for the Philippian Christians, he said, "And this I pray, that your love may abound yet more and more in knowledge and in all judgment; That ye may approve things that are excellent" (Philippians 1:9, 10).

Man's knowledge of the character of a holy life and the power to live a holy life is determined by the intensity of his love for a holy God.

DEC. 11 Perhaps there have been a few secret believers in every generation — men and women who for one reason or another have never publicly declared their allegiance to Jesus Christ. However, the exhortation of Scripture is that Christians should raise the flag and let the world know where they stand and what they stand for.

"For the scripture saith, whosoever believeth on him shall not be ashamed" (Romans 10:11).

To a multitude of people whose religion had become anemic and whose confession was almost non-existent Jesus said, "Let your light so shine before men, that they may see your good works, and glorify your Father which is in heaven" (Matthew 5:16).

DEC. 12 The Gospel is being preached to more people today than in any other generation that has ever lived. This is adequate cause for rejoicing in the Christian church, because the Bible says that "the gospel is the power of God unto salvation to everyone that believeth" (Romans 1:16).

Men may differ over the manner and the sponsorship of the preaching but the glorious fact remains that Christ is being preached in a needy world.

There were some preachers in New Testament days who were not sincere, but from his prison in Rome, Paul rejoiced in the fact that the message was going out. "What then? notwithstanding, every way, whether in pretence, or in truth, Christ is preached; and I therein do rejoice, yea, and will rejoice" (Philippians 1:18).

What a tragedy it would be to live in this generation of great gospel preaching and hear the message without responding to it and accepting the claims of Christ.

DEC. 13 In every Christian home the wall of good example must be built. Our children learn a great deal more from watching what we do than from doing what we say.

What our children become twenty years from now will be determined to a large extent by what we are today. Parents who are godly will usually produce children who go in the same direction. Parents who have no time for God themselves cannot expect any more from their children.

The Bible says, "Train up a child in the way he should go: and when he is old, he will not depart from it" (Proverbs 22:6).

DEC. 14 There are two kinds of separation. There is separation from the world and there is separation unto God.

It is possible to be separated from the world and not separated unto God. Some people boast of a negative religious life. There are many things they do not do, but often these same people demonstrate little of the love of Christ in their lives. They are separated from some of the things in the world, but they are not in close contact with God.

The major thrust of the Bible is not that a man should concentrate upon withdrawing himself from the world, but that he should bend every effort to live as close to God as possible.

The Apostle told the Christians at Rome that he was "separated unto the gospel of God" (Romans 1:1).

The Bible says, "What doth the Lord thy God require of thee, but to fear the Lord thy God, to walk in all his ways, and to love him, and to serve the Lord thy God with all thy heart and with all thy soul" (Deuteronomy 10:12)?

DEC. 15 Christianity involves a personal contact with the living Lord. It is not the adoption of a good religion. It is not assent to a set of beliefs. It is not an attempt to live up to a high code of ethics. It is an infusion by a divine miracle of the life of God into the life of man.

When a man commits his life to God through faith in Christ, he becomes a part of the living church, a stone in the living building, a member of the living body, a branch grafted into the living vine.

Jesus said, "I am the vine, ye are the branches: He that abideth in me, and I in him, the same bringeth forth much fruit: for without me ye can do nothing" (John 15:5).

DEC. 16 When Isaiah prophesied the birth of Jesus he called Him "The Prince of Peace" and when the angels announced His arrival to the shepherds they predicted "peace on earth, good will toward men."

But when Jesus spoke for Himself He said, "Think not that I am come to send peace on earth: I came not to send peace, but a sword" (Matthew 10:34).

This seems to be a contradiction until we read John's account: "He was in the world, and the world knew him not. He came unto his own; and his own received him not" (John 1:10, 11).

The world rejected the Prince of Peace but hundreds of individuals in the world accepted Him. These people know the peace of God in their hearts, but because of their loyalty to Christ they are divided, as by a sword, from unbelievers.

The Bible promises the Second Coming of Christ and the establishment of His Kingdom in the world and the reality of "Peace on Earth." Those who have trusted Christ have already experienced this in their personal lives.

DEC. 17   The Psalmist referred to the Bible as "a lamp unto my feet, and a light unto my path" (Psalm 119:105).

Most people lose their way spiritually because they let the light go out in their lives. They lose contact with the Word of God. It is difficult for a Christian to be a consistent reader of the Bible and at the same time live a life of sin. If a man is living outside of the will of God, the Bible will convict him of his sin and make him miserable until he gets right with God.

If a man is living for God, he is not afraid to open the Word and let the searchlight of Divine inspiration penetrate every area of his life.

The Bible says, "But he that doeth truth cometh to the light, that his deeds may be made manifest, that they are wrought in God" (John 3:21).

DEC. 18   A suit of clothes would be worthless if it did not go with the man and comply with his every movement.

When the man raises his arm, the suit must raise its arm. When the man sits down, the suit must sit down. When the man walks, the suit must walk.

The Bible pictures the Christian as a suit in which Christ lives. He is a man whose activities and words and thoughts are directed by the indwelling Christ. One of the apostles said, "For me to live is Christ" (Philippians 1:21). His life was so dedicated to God that his body had become a temple through which the living Lord contacted the world.

"Know ye not that ye are the temple of God, and that the Spirit of God dwelleth in you?" (I Corinthians 3:16).

Christianity is a total submission to God through faith in His Son that makes a man a physical suit in which the Spirit of God dwells.

DEC. 19 There are times when the burdened back of the suffering Christian becomes a stepping stone by which the Gospel is carried into hearts that could not have been reached in any other way.

When the Apostle Paul was imprisoned in Rome, it looked as if his long treacherous voyage to the imperial city had been in vain. He could not walk the streets and enter the houses of the Romans to tell them the message of the Gospel. He was bound, and apparently at the end of his usefulness.

However, he had lived for God long enough to know that his imprisonment was not without purpose. He said, "I would ye should understand, brethren, that the things which happened unto me have fallen out rather unto the furtherance of the gospel; So that my bonds in Christ are manifest in all the palace, and in all other places" (Philippians 1:12, 13).

DEC. 20 Every Christian needs to surround himself with a wall of discipline that makes it difficult to yield to temptation.

If a man would be saved from the smudge of sin, if he would be freed from the fear of falling, if he would be untroubled in the trial of temptation, he must put himself as often as possible into circumstances in life where it is difficult for him to sin.

When Paul wrote to Timothy he said, "Flee also youthful lusts: but follow righteousness, faith, charity, peace, with them that call on the Lord out of a pure heart" (II Timothy 2:22).

There is enough trouble with temptation in a well-regulated life. How much more dangerous it is to remove the regulations and to be compromised by a position where it is easy to sin.

DEC. 21 In four days it will be Christmas, and the thing that thrills us is that most of the civilized world stops in its tracks to celebrate the birth of Jesus Christ.

This is wonderful, but how much better it is for those who not only celebrate His birth but know Him as a personal Saviour.

This is the message of Christmas. The Bible says, "The Son of man came not to be ministered unto, but to minister, and to give his life a ransom for many" (Matthew 20:28). May God grant that each one of us will commit out lives to God through faith in Christ and know by experience the meaning of Christmas because we have been ransomed.

DEC. 22 In a few days it will be Christmas. We think back to an historical fact — the birth of a human baby in Bethlehem — a baby who grew to manhood, eating and drinking and sleeping and weeping along with the rest of mankind.

But the Babe of Bethlehem was far superior to other men. He lived His life without sin and founded a religion that has endured nearly two thousand years.

But we miss the whole point of the Christmas message if we do not lift our eyes beyond the humanity of Christ and see Him as God — God in human form. The Bible says, "Behold, a virgin shall be with child, and shall bring forth a son, and they shall call his name Emmanuel, which being interpreted is, God with us" (Matthew 1:23).

DEC. 23   It will soon be Christmas. All of us will benefit by the holidays and gifts and good times that this day brings, but there are many who will not know what it is all about. They will know that Christ was born, but they will not realize why He was born.

He was a good man, a great teacher, a healer of diseases, and a leader of men, but the Bible makes it clear that He was born to die. He came into this world to die for the sins of mankind. Jesus said, "And as Moses lifted up the serpent in the wilderness, even so must the Son of Man be lifted up: That whosoever believeth in him should not perish, but have eternal life" (John 3:14, 15).

DEC. 24   This is Christmas Eve — we hustle here and there and in the back of our minds are the questions: "Is everything done? Have I forgotten anything? Am I ready for the great day?"

We should be ready for Christmas — not only materially but spiritually. If we are to adequately celebrate the birth of our Lord, we should be in fellowship with Him. We should be able to greet Christmas morning knowing that our sins are forgiven, we are right with God, and we are on our way to heaven.

What a tragedy it would be to carry our sins into the Christmas celebrations when it is so easy to be forgiven. The Bible says, "If we confess our sins, he is faithful and just to forgive us our sins, and to cleanse us from all unrighteousness" (I John 1:9).

**DEC.
25**
On Christmas we celebrate the day the Wise Men came to worship the Christ where He lay in a manger. They came, and after they had seen Him they "returned another way."

No one is quite the same after he has come into contact with Christ. We come to Him one way — with our sins and heartaches and human failures. We go out another way — with our sins forgiven, His peace in our hearts, and an everlasting hope before us.

The Bible says, "But God, who is rich in mercy . . . Even when we were dead in sins, hath quickened us together with Christ . . . And hath raised us up together and made us sit together in heavenly places in Christ Jesus" (Ephesians 2:4-6).

**DEC.
26**
In the entire lifetime there may be only one person whom we know intimately. This is the result of a long friendship during which two lives have been so interwoven that they become almost inseparable. Everything has been shared in the complete confidence of intimate friendship.

When the Bible speaks of knowing God through faith in Christ, this is what it means. Christianity involves a relationship with the Son of God in which His life has become a part of our lives and our lives have been lost in His.

This is not a long distance relationship or a casual Sunday observance. It is an intimate communion that is closer than any human tie. This is the knowledge of God that opens our eyes to a new day and says: "Good morning, Lord." This is the awareness of His presence throughout every activity of the day. This is the personal fellowship with Jesus that turns out the lights and says, "Good night, Lord."

This is what the Apostle Paul meant when he said, "That I may know him" (Philippians 3:10). This is Christianity.

DEC. 27 The Old Testament tells us that David was a man after God's own heart, he began the line of kings through which Jesus came into the world, and he was one of the inspired writers of Scripture.

However, most people also know that David committed a crime so desperate that decent people blush to talk of it. David was a mountain peak among Old Testament characters, but he sinned and needed to be forgiven.

Let the moral guard of the most stalwart of modern spiritual giants be lowered but for a moment and he becomes an easy target for the flat smooth stone from the sling shot of Satan's stripling.

The Bible says, "Be sober, be vigilant, because your adversary the devil, as a roaring lion, walketh about, seeking whom he may devour" (I Peter 5:8).

DEC. 28 The righteous man carves his name upon the rock and it lasts forever. The wicked man writes his name in the sand and the sea of time washes his remembrance into oblivion.

The man of God ploughs his furrows in the solid earth of faith in Christ and reaps a harvest that is eternal. The man of the world ploughs his furrows in the sea. He may leave a brilliant trail that sparkles for a moment, but the waves roll over it as if it had never been there.

The Psalmist said, "The way of the ungodly shall perish," and about the righteous man he said, "Whatsoever he doeth shall prosper" (Psalm 1:6, 3).

Even the most glorious deeds of the sinner will perish, but the most humble deeds of the saint will prosper.

DEC. 29
The most important of all names is "Jesus." The Bible says, "Wherefore God also hath highly exalted him, and given him a name which is above every name" (Philippians 2:9).

"Jesus" is a Greek rendition of the Hebrew name Joshua, and it means "Jehovah is Salvation." Joshua was only a partial fulfillment of his own name. He led his people out of the wilderness and into the Promised Land.

In Jesus God came into the world of men and paid the price that actually saved us from our sin. This was the promise of the angel to Joseph, and now it is impossible for a person to recognize Jesus without admitting his own sin. His name, "Jesus," forever points to the sin of man and the salvation of God.

DEC. 30
The man whom Jesus described as a fool in the gospel of Luke was obviously a respectable citizen. The person who lives riotously and immorally will not be the successful farmer that this man was.

He was the kind of individual that would add prestige and dignity to any lodge or club or church. His signature would give a man a position.

He was respectable but he was not righteous. Respectability is often mistaken for righteousness, but it is merely human righteousness which the Bible says is "as filthy rags."

The Apostle Paul said, "But what things were gain to me, those I counted loss for Christ" (Philippians 3:7).

The man who mistakes his respectability for righteousness is a fool in the eyes of God.

DEC. 31 Sin is a desperate thing. All the war, all the crime, and all the heartaches in life are the result of sin. Sin produces alcoholics, builds penitentiaries, and fills mental hospitals. Sin dissipates the eye, destroys the mind and dooms the soul.

All broken homes and displaced children and ruined lives have been manufactured in the factories of sin.

Sin is the saddest thing in the world. Sin is the great human tragedy. Sin is the dilemma of mankind. Everyone is a part of this sadness, an actor in this tragedy, an element in this dilemma until he comes to Jesus Christ and his sins are forgiven. This is what happened to one man many years ago when Jesus said, "Son, be of good cheer; thy sins be forgiven thee" (Matthew 9:2). This is what happens to us when we trust Christ as our Saviour.